Hazel Hale-Bostic's **Harvesting Memories** is truly a treasure to those of us Southwest Virginians who cannot let go of our own Appalachian heritage.

Like a skilled archaeologist, Hazel excavates the bones of our heritage in order to capture and share the true essence of our past.

Whether you are a browser, in depth reader, or just an information junkie you will find something on every page of **Harvesting Memories** that will shine a light on our proud history.

Dr. Bob Sutherland
Dean of Learning Resources
Southwest Virginia Community College

Harvesting Memories recounts simpler times when money was scarce, but where, in the coal mining hills of Virginia, family and community were everything. Stories that define the region, both poignant and funny, Ms. Bostic shares a wonderful walk down memory lane.

Ms. Bostic has won several People's Choice Awards through *The Storyteller Magazine*, a sure sign that her stories touch on our own memories that make us laugh and cry—occasionally at the same time.

This is a book I would recommend for everyone.

Regina Williams, Editor
The Storyteller Magazine

Swords Creek
Hale Raisin'

Wheelchair Angel

From my paternal grandmother, Ida Belle Breedlove Hale, I learned to love hot tea, Cream of Wheat, and Jesus Christ.

I was a very small child when Granny came to live with us. She'd had her right leg amputated due to diabetes, and being widowed, was unable to care for herself. She was also mother of ten children, and during the early 1950s the dreaded words "nursing home" were rarely uttered. Families took care of their elderly.

I loved it when it was "our turn" to keep Granny. My first memory of her was riding in her large wheelchair. I'd climb up in her lap, and we'd roll into the dining room and enjoy our breakfast together. Inevitably, it consisted of Cream of Wheat and hot tea. I felt grownup having my own cup of tea, even if it was half milk.

After breakfast, we'd roll into the living room, and sit by the double windows. She'd always look up, and even as a child, I sensed a change in her. Her face glowed, and she smiled.

I'd ask, "Granny, what do you see up there?"

"Why, child," she'd answer, "I see Jesus waiting for me to come home."

This bothered me because I didn't want her to leave, and I'd ask lots more questions. Granny patiently answered, and told me about this man, Jesus. She said He lived in Heaven with his Father, and if we lived good lives we could someday go to be with Him. She described Heaven in such vivid detail, that today, years later, I imagine it being a city of pure gold with walls of jasper.

A place where day never ends, whose pure river of life flows endlessly, and the tree of life never dies.

She also made me realize that I was special by telling me that God, the Father of Jesus, had made just one of me. She explained that God put each one of us on this earth to do what only we as individuals could do. She said we were to trust Him and obey Him when he revealed what this job might be. Granny never grew tired of talking about her Savior, and I never grew tired of listening to her.

My dad and mom were not Christian people at that time. This greatly troubled Granny, but she never scolded or talked mean to them. She'd say things like, "Son, I could die a lot easier knowing that you and Effie were saved."

I'd then ask, "Granny, am I saved?"

She'd smile her gentle smile and tell me, "Yes, darlin', you are a child, and God has you in his arms." Try as I might, I couldn't feel God's arms around me, but Granny said so, and that was good enough for me.

I'd spend hours with Granny, and Mom worried that I was aggravating her, but Granny said I was good company. She'd play dolls with me, and allow me to comb her hair, and didn't even fuss when I smeared Mom's red lipstick on her. But her favorite time was sharing Bible stories. She not only enjoyed it, but looking back I believe she felt that since her son and daughter-in-law didn't take me to church, it was imperative that she teach me the plan of salvation. I'm sure she asked God for guidance so that she might explain it all to a young child. Her lessons stuck with me, but the way she lived; her actions, showed me even more.

The fall of 1952, I entered first grade. I was excited, but didn't want to leave Granny. By then, she was practically staying full time with us. My maternal grandmother, Ada Combs, was there too, and she was of great help to Mom.

4

The first day of school found me all dressed up in a new Sears dress and Tiller's Department Store shoes. Both grandmothers said I was just about the prettiest thing they'd ever seen, and Granny Hale called me to her side. She bowed her head, and asked the Lord to watch over me and keep me safe throughout the day. She did this every morning, but one particular morning in early May, Granny was too sick to leave her bed. I wanted to see her before leaving for school, but Mom said she was too sick to be bothered.

I didn't feel right leaving for school without first praying with Granny.

Our house was located close enough to school so that we were able to walk home for lunch. Occasionally, Mom gave us money so that we could stop by Artie Rickman's store on our return walk. Artie's store was located on the opposite side of the road from the school. Of course, we always looked both ways before crossing the road. That day I had bought a banana Popsicle, and was trudging along, my mind on Granny because she was still in bed during lunchtime.

The next thing I knew, people were crowding around me, and I was lying in the middle of the highway, hurting. I had walked out in front of H. L. and Corrine Dye's car. I'd been hit so hard, I'd turned three flips on the hardtop, but I held on to that banana Popsicle!

H. L. was paralyzed with fear as he carefully examined me. The cars built in 1952 were heavy vehicles, and his car had just struck a small six-year-old child. After determining there were no broken bones, he lifted me and placed me on the back seat of his car. He and Corrine were amazed I wasn't crying. I don't remember feeling afraid. I just wondered what all the fuss was about.

He and Corrine took me home, and begged Mom and Dad to allow them to drive me to the hospital. Dad said, "There's no need. She seems all right." I was very sore and bruised, but back then, if a person wasn't drawing his last breath, hospitals were dismissed as nonsense.

H. L. and Corrine reluctantly left, and I got in bed with Granny. She placed her small frail hand on my head, and I went to sleep knowing that all was well if she was beside me.

It turned out that at precisely the same time I was hit by the car, Granny was praying, asking God to watch over me. She told Mom that she and I hadn't prayed that morning, and she felt a need to pray.

Granny Hale died two years later, June 1954. It's been a long time, but I miss her still. And I often wonder if Mom had allowed Granny to pray for me on that day in May, would the accident have happened? Or if Granny was warned, since she was praying when the car struck me. Was this why I wasn't seriously injured or even killed?

I've no concrete evidence that I've had experience with spiritual beings, but physical, living, breathing ones, I won't hesitate to tell you—yes, my Granny Hale was indeed one of God's own precious angels.

Granny Hale with grandchildren Buddy, Linda, T.J., Sandy, Roger, Wayne and me. I'm the one standing beside Granny wearing a circle-tail dress, lace-up patent leather shoes and a frown. I didn't like sharing Granny. Swords Creek, 1950

Remembering Granny Combs

I was only four, but I have a vivid memory of "dancing at the end of a switch," and Granny Combs was calling the tune.

She was staying with us at the time to help Mom with the new baby. It was May 1950, and on this particular beautiful day, I had decided to go visiting—in other words, I had slipped off.

Granny looked and looked for me until she was frantic. Finally, she spotted my blonde head peeping around one of our neighbor's porch posts.

"Hazel!" she hollered, "you come on home!"

I stepped from behind the post, rared back like a big rooster, and yelled, "You get back in that house, you old shit ass, you!"

Boy, I felt so proud. I showed that old woman—she wasn't about to tell me what to do!

I didn't feel proud for long. All I felt was the sting of a little keen switch.

So begins my storehouse of "Granny Memories."

Born Ada Mae Alice Craft in 1892, in Glen Lyn, Virginia, Granny Combs was the youngest of 18 children. Her parents were poor and sold her at age 10 to a wealthy family who trained her to be a children's nurse. She stayed with this family until age 15, and was then sent to Big A Mountain in Russell County, Virginia, to work as a nurse for Dr. Johnson Combs.

She eventually married one of his sons, William Johnson Combs. She was 16, and he was 36.

Years later, when my grandfather died, Granny was still fairly young. Traveling by bus or train, she divided her time between her five children. She was always on the go, but our place was home base for her.

While she was away on one of her many trips, Dad changed the back porch steps from the side to the center of the porch. I remember Granny arrived back "home" late one afternoon, and no one thought to tell her about the steps. Night had fallen, and Granny was on her way to the toilet. She stepped off on what used to be the steps and sailed into midair. When we found her, she was all sprawled out, moaning. She never forgot that near visit to "Johnny."

A jolly, happy person, Granny made people laugh. She looked about as round as she was tall, which was just over five feet. She took the bus to town every Saturday she stayed with us. Honaker was a few miles away, and she'd spend the entire day visiting the local merchants. Walter and Rush Gent, owners of a hardware store, paid Granny to come in their store to sit in a rocking chair and talk with their customers. Rush later told me Granny was a much bigger drawing card than any sale they could have had.

It was while rocking and talking that Granny met Mr. Lockhart. He asked Granny for a date, and the two agreed that he would ride up to Swords Creek the following Saturday on the 4 p.m. bus. Later, one of his children would drive up and take him back home.

Granny began preparations for this momentous occasion early that day. She shampooed her hair, even used her new hair combs to style it. She wore her nicest dress, the one with the white collar, and pinned on her cameo brooch. She was ready an hour before the bus was due.

"Well, while I'm waiting, I may as well feed the chickens," she said.

The chicken house was down the road by some property Dad rented out to Jack Cartwright. In those days, many people still bathed in galvanized tubs and threw the bath water out the back door. Dressed in her Sunday best, Granny rounded the corner of the chicken house precisely at the moment Jack Cartwright let fly with a tubful of dirty water!

Her beautiful dress, hair, shoes and brooch were drenched. She trudged back home, carrying her little basket, now filled with wet chicken feed. She was crying, and the tears made white streaks through the black on her face. My sister Frankie and I decided if having a date could do all this to a person, we wouldn't be in any hurry to have one of our own.

Granny was so embarrassed she canceled the date. Mr. Lockhart was persistent, though, and visited again. He and Granny remained friends for years.

Granny also loved bright colors, especially pink, and had a green thumb—she could put anything in a pot of dirt and it would grow. The summer I turned 13, she decided to paint all 30 of her flower buckets pink. I helped. We painted and painted. After we'd finished, there was paint left over.

Granny said to me, "You know, I think I'll paint your dad's dog houses."

"Don't do it, Granny! He'll kill you!"

"He'll just have to kill," she calmly replied, "because I'm going to. You going to help me?"

"No way," I answered.

I'll never forget how ridiculous Dad's hound dogs looked poking their heads out of pink dog houses! When Dad came home from work, I don't know what was loudest, his cursing or Granny's laughter.

Granny Combs was 70 years old when she passed away on June 14, 1962. Because of rough beginnings, she might have

11

become embittered, but instead she chose to enjoy life and leave us a wonderful legacy of love.

Ada Mae Alice Craft Combs (Granny)

Uncle Arthur's Toothache

Everyone fondly called him "Uncle Arthur." Arthur Davis and his wife, Betty, lived at the bottom of our hill in Swords Creek, Virginia.

I could lie across a bed in an upstairs bedroom of our house and look down on the Davis house. The two-story colonial with its wraparound porch, lush lawn, imposing oaks and lilac bushes was just the kind of home I dreamed of owning one day.

Uncle Arthur was a well-educated man who served as the local justice of the peace. He was also so accommodating that he once unhitched his team of horses from the plow and loaned them to a neighbor.

Those of us who lived on the hill got water from a reservoir that was fed by a spring. But during dry spells, the spring quit flowing and there wasn't enough water.

When that happened, the generous Uncle Arthur freely shared his well water. That was the case one hot summer day in 1953 when I met Dad at the foot of the hill. As he stepped off the miners' bus, I yelled, "Dad, we ain't got no water!"

"Well," Dad replied, "I guess we'd better go home and fetch some water jugs. Your mother won't let me in the house wearing all this coal dust."

We got the jugs and started across the field to the Davis house. Uncle Arthur was standing on the back porch, wearing what appeared to be a pillowcase on his head and waving his arms.

"Whoa, Beauchamp!" he yelled to my father, "Whoa, Beauchamp!"

As we reached the porch, we could see Uncle Arthur's face was swollen and his eyes red-rimmed. His hair was standing on end, and he looked haggard.

Uncle Arthur was always neat, pleasant and easygoing, so it was a shock to see him in this agitated state.

"Uncle Arthur," Dad asked. "What in the world is wrong?"

"You've got to help me," he replied. "I've had a toothache for the past three days. You've *got* to pull the tooth!"

"I'll do no such thing," Dad protested. "You have an infection, and I'd be afraid to touch it."

Then Aunt Betty came to the door, wringing her hands on a large white apron. "I'll help you," she pleaded. "I've been up with him for the past three nights, and I'm about dead."

Dad finally agreed. So Aunt Betty quickly found some string, and Uncle Arthur sat in a straight-backed chair on the porch. Dad tied one end of the string around the tooth and wrapped the other around his right hand.

Bracing his foot against the bottom rung of the chair, Dad looked at Uncle Arthur and asked, "Are you *sure* about this?" The poor man just rolled his eyes and nodded his heavily wrapped head.

After a "practice run," Dad braced all his weight and, using his full strength, pulled straight up.

He jerked the tooth—and Uncle Arthur—right out of that chair. The chair hit the floor with a bang at the same time Uncle Arthur did.

Uncle Arthur sat up, screamed like a banshee, grabbed his jaw and began running around the house. Dad and Aunt Betty, her apron flapping in the breeze, ran after him. I hid behind one of the lilac bushes.

Then Uncle Arthur stopped as suddenly as he began. He grabbed Dad, hugged him and shook his hand.

"Thank you, Beauchamp, thank you," he said. "I've never felt better."

With that, Uncle Arthur walked back to the porch, where we left him sleeping peacefully on the glider.

As Dad and I walked up the hill toward home, pulling my red wagon full of water jugs, Dad grinned and said, "At least we'll save on water tonight. Arthur Davis scared the coal dust right off me. I'll bet I'm as white as a sheet."

Arthur and Betty Davis

My coal miner Dad

Saddle Oxfords and Grapevine Swings

My mother had warned me, "You take that baby to the grapevine swings, and if your daddy don't wear you out, I will!"

"Baby," I snorted as I ran, pulling my four-year-old sister, Frankie, by her hand. Nobody called me baby, I thought. I kicked gravel with the toe of my black-and-white saddle oxfords. Then I quickly checked for scuff marks, and fastened a back buckle. These shoes were finally on my feet after months of waiting until Mom's egg and butter money built up.

I looked back at my best friend, July Belcher. She had her four-year-old brother, Sonny, by his hand too. She jerked rather than pulled Sonny along behind her. Her auburn hair bounced, and a frown replaced her wide smile.

Judy and Sonny lived with their grandparents, Bert and Laura Vance, in the house below us, and from the time they arrived, Judy and I practically stayed together. However, it was our misfortune to always have to care for the "babies." We couldn't go anyplace without them. Once there, we couldn't really do anything because all our time and attention were focused on them. It was enough to make seven-year-olds want to leave home — for good.

Judy and I had planned for days to ride the grapevines on Jack Cartwright's property in Call Valley in the next hollow above us. All our friends would be there. Yesterday, when we asked Mom and Laura's permission, we were told we must watch the children. No amount of begging changed their minds. We added a few

17

tears, but Mom and Laura sternly warned us to stay away from the swings. They chorused, "It's way too dangerous, and we need you home to watch the children while we work the gardens."

Mom included her warning, "You take that baby to the grapevine swings, and if your daddy don't wear you out, I will!"

Laura had pointed her finger at Judy, and in her George Patton voice said, "Young lady, the same goes for you."

So today, while Mom and Laura stood underneath the apple trees in Laura's yard enjoying a much needed break from garden work, I had looked at Judy and pointed toward Call Valley. She nodded in agreement, so we grabbed Frankie and Sonny. Mom and Laura were too engrossed in swapping the latest gossip to realize we'd walked across neighbor Stella Stiltner's yard, crawled through a hole in her fence, and were now on our way to joining our friends.

We were almost there, so close we could hear squeals of delight. We quickened our pace, excitement mounting. Then we heard something above the laughter. Judy stopped in her tracks, and Sonny plowed into her. He let out a yelp, but Judy silenced him by clapping a hand over his mouth. It was Mom and Laura! They were not far behind us, and closing in fast.

We immediately detoured to another route home. Frankie and Sonny were exhausted, and set up cries of protest. I kept thinking where to hide to save our hides.

It seemed we reached home in record time, but we were ready to again take flight when we spied Mom and Laura struggling to cross Stella's fence that separated her property from the Cartwrights.' I prayed they'd get tangled up and fall, but they maneuvered like soldiers on a mission.

We left Frankie and Sonny standing under the apple trees, warned them if they told we'd strangle them, and headed for the cellar underneath Laura's house.

We got as far back as possible, behind the potato bin — completely hidden. It was dark and cool, and we were able to breathe deeply and calm our racing hearts. Still I felt like a mouse being chased by a cat.

I heard the cat yell, "Hazel, you get out here right this minute! Do you hear me, Hazel Loretta?"

Laura chimed in, "Judith Wilma Belcher, I'll skin you alive!"

There we stood completely frozen to the dirt floor. God help us, we heard the cellar door open.

I heard Mom say to Laura, "I see something black-and-white behind the potato bin!"

I quickly pulled my feet in, but too late. My shoes had given us away.

We were yanked outside, Mom and Laura scolding in unison, "Didn't we warn you to stay away from the swings? You could have gotten the babies and yourselves killed."

I could see the "babies" were thoroughly enjoying all this.

Mom broke off about three apple tree limbs, at least they felt like limbs to me. Then she did just what she'd promised. She wore me out. I danced right out of my black-and-white saddle oxfords.

Judy and I passed each other as we were slung around trying to dodge those awful switches. Judy never whimpered. She was too stubborn. Not me! I used more than one of Daddy's choice curse words. The more I yelled and cursed, the harder Mom applied punishment.

The news media had quite a field day some years ago reporting "caning" incidents in Singapore.

I could tell the media a thing or two. For me, caning began that summer of 1953. I never pass an apple tree that I don't remember it. A woman named Judy who lives in Butler, Ohio, remembers it too.

Me and "the baby"

Warm Morning Memories

It had become a favorite ritual. Granny (Ada) Combs and I arose each Saturday morning to allow Mom and Dad the luxury of sleeping in. This made Granny feel useful and needed. She was independent and wanted to pay her way. Grandpa Combs had died several years earlier and I don't think she felt comfortable living with her children, no matter how extended the welcome. I'd hear her telling Mom, "You know, I never had much, but Lord, how I miss my own house. It's never the same once you break up housekeeping."

Mom hastened to reassure Granny, telling her how much we enjoyed having her.

Granny couldn't help feeling because she was older she had a perfect right to tell others what to do. Dad was always telling us *he* was head of the household, so he and Granny frequently clashed. When Dad called her "Little General," Granny sulked several days and refused to eat at the same table with him. We knew a truce had been called when Granny opened her sewing basket and sewed already stable buttons on Dad's work shirts. I never once heard her apologize. She just quietly slipped on her thimble and loudly proclaimed Dad's shirts a mess.

One cold February morning in 1953, Granny's headstrong streak almost proved to be her undoing. As with many households during this time, we heated our home with coal and wood. The cook stove dominated our small kitchen, while a Warm Morning heater sat in the living room. It stood about five feet tall, and its

21

covering was brown metal with grill work. There was a grate in the bottom, and below the grate was an ash pan. A door opened in front for loading coal and wood. Another access to the stove's interior was an opening on top.

Dad had house rules concerning our stoves. Only he was allowed to "bank" the fires each night, and start them the following morning. I secretly called Dad "Fire Lord."

On this Saturday morning the Fire Lord and his Lady slept peacefully in our one downstairs bedroom. I was sitting on the wide arm of an imitation velvet-covered chair in the living room watching Granny as she opened the top door of the Warm Morning.

Granny was dressed in a cotton housedress, and her standard two-pocket apron was tied securely around her oversized waist. Her hair was twisted neatly into a bun at her nape.

Granny wore sandals year-round unless the ground was snow-covered. Today, her lace-up, open-toe, open-heel blacks looked especially shiny. I asked, "Granny, how did you get your shoes so shiny?"

Granny was bending over to get the ash-covered poker. As she grasped it, she turned around to look at me and the poker almost caught me upside my head. I knew she meant no harm, but Granny had a habit of gesturing. As she waved the poker, ashes going everywhere, she said, "Why, honey, I've told you before. Just split a leftover biscuit in half and rub your shoes. Best shine in the world!"

My childlike mind bounced around in all directions, so I was soon off that subject. Besides, I'd just missed having a knot raised by that evil-looking poker, so I asked, "What are you doing with that thing?"

Granny raised her head. She'd been standing on tiptoe to look inside the stove. "I'm going to stir up this fire if you'd quit asking so many questions. You're nothing but a question box. Have to know everything, don't you? And Hazel, keep your voice down! Let your mom and dad sleep a while. They're wore out."

"But Granny, you're not supposed to start the fire. Dad said . . . "

"I know what *Dad* said. You'd think I'd never seen a stove the way he carries on. Why I was building fires before Beach Hale was ever heard of."

"Granny, Dad never uses that poker. He just shakes the grate. I know 'cause he lets me help sometimes."

I was ignored as Granny again stood on tiptoe, leaned way over, her head now completely immersed in the stove, and began punching and gouging with the poker.

The noise awakened Dad in the next room and he yelled, "Adie, I'll do that. Leave it alone!"

Granny opened her mouth to reply when — boom! The stove appeared to rise several inches off the floor.

The stovepipe disconnected from the wall. Smoke, fire, and soot shot from the stove into the air and Granny fell back on the couch. Dad jumped to the floor and came running, his long johns flapping. I ran around the room screaming. Granny's hair was burning. Fire!

Dad jerked Granny's ruffle-tail apron over her face and smothered the flames.

"Oh Beach! Oh Lord!" moaned Granny.

"Don't you 'Oh Beach' me, Adie! I *told* you not to mess with that stove. Hazel, run to the kitchen, wet a towel, and bring it to your granny."

I grabbed a large dishtowel, poured water over it and ran to Granny. I had failed to wring out the rag, and water pooled on her dress.

Spluttering, Granny came up for air. "Well, why don't you just take me to the horse trough!" she yelled at Dad.

"I know where I'd like to take you," he growled. Then he looked straight at her. "Adie, you sure won't need to worry about chin hairs. You can put away that little hand mirror and tweezers. There's not a hair on your face. You don't even have hair in your nose."

Dad pulled me onto his lap and laughed until he shook.

I giggled and giggled while Granny stood on shaky legs and moved slowly toward the kitchen. Dad nudged me. "Go with your Granny. Keep an eye on her while I tackle this mess."

I stood just inside the kitchen and observed Granny as she looked at herself in the oval mirror hanging above the sink. It would take more than a wet dishtowel to remove all that grime. She looked like a frightened raccoon. Her face was completely black except for the white circles where her glasses had been. Her wire-framed glasses had been blown off her face and were now at the bottom of the stove. Her eyebrows and eyelashes were gone. Her hair was scorched and there were bald spots, red angry places requiring immediate attention. Tears sprang to her eyes as she dabbed Cloverine salve on the spots.

My eyes slowly traveled from this horrid sight to her shoes. They were a mess—ashes, soot and black smoke combined with biscuit grease.

Dad insisted Granny clean herself and get to bed. For once, she didn't argue. He worked hard to get things in order, but Mom's prized criss-cross Priscilla curtains were filthy as were the living room wall, scatter rugs, and lamp shades.

Thanks to a heavy dose of red "nerve medicine" Mom had taken the night before, she had slept through the whole thing. When her alarm sounded and she stepped out of the bedroom into the living room, she glanced around but said not a word. She reached into a pocket of her chenille robe, pulled out the nerve medicine, tipped it to her mouth and took a hefty swallow. Then she rolled up her sleeves and went to work.

Upstairs Granny opened a door and yelled, "Hazel, bring me some of your mom's nerve medicine!"

Dad, working to reinstate the stove pipe, said, "Adie, save some for me!"

Granny and niece Geraldine Vance

Fox Hunting—
A Family Tradition

Too excited to sleep, I sat in the middle of my bed. This April morning was unlike any other morning. As the night gave way to soft pink, and the sun peeped over the mountains surrounding my Southwest Virginia home, I asked myself, "How can I convince Dad to take me fox hunting? I've just got to hear that new dog."

Heck, he hadn't even arrived, but already he was my hero. I'd even named him. Twice. An extraordinary dog shouldn't have an ordinary name, so I'd given him a double name, George Alan.

"If you're going to the train station with your dad, get dressed," Mom called to me. Throwing on jeans, shirt, and tennis shoes, I tore down the stairs.

Traveling to the depot, I asked Dad hunting questions.

"When is the best time to hunt?"

Surprised and pleased at my interest in the sport that was an obsession with him, he answered eagerly.

"The best time to hunt is when the ground is damp; scent is on the ground. And, you don't want to hunt on a windy night, because the wind drowns the dog's barking."

"How do you know your dogs?"

"Each dog has a different 'mouth,' some finer, some course, and some in between. There's no two exactly alike. It takes a few races to learn them, and if a fellow is tone deaf, he should never fox hunt."

"How many dogs do you need in a race?"

"No more than six, because if there's too many it's difficult to identify your dogs. Fewer numbers make for a better race."

"Dad, I've heard you complain about people 'throwing in' on a race. What does this mean?"

"Let me explain — say my dogs have started the race, and have been running hard for an hour or so. If someone throws in 'fresh' dogs, my dogs are too worn out to compete, and just quit. Once a foxhound quits, that's it. A valuable dog becomes invaluable."

The train depot was coming in sight, so I stopped the questions. As we waited for the crate containing the prized Oklahoma dog to be unloaded, I pictured a black and tan Walker hound. When the depot agent opened the crate, I saw he was a Walker all right, but the ugliest lemon-spotted, yellow-eyed dog I'd ever seen.

Dad questioned the agent, "Are you sure you have the name correct? Any other dogs on that train?"

The agent answered, "Sir, like him or not, he's yours."

The three of us made a sad picture as we departed — a hound that should have been black and tan, but wasn't, a teary-eyed 10-year-old girl, and a foxhunter who looked as if he had just lost the race.

Several weeks passed before I had enough courage to approach Dad about hunting. If only he would allow me to go on one hunt with him, I could convince him that I was as tough as any old boy. Besides, I'd already stood in front of my fifth grade classmates and made the grand announcement, "I'm going fox hunting with my dad!"

He was busy preparing his carbide light, and I sidled up to him and asked, "Dad, know what I want for my birthday?"

Setting his flask down on the wooden table, Dad, home from a grueling day of mining coal, wearily asked, "No, Hazel, what do you want?"

"I want to go hunting with you, and I want to lead George Alan."

I was totally surprised when a smile lit his coal-blackened face. "Sounds good to me, but what's your mother going to say?"

Mom said "NO," until I convinced Marie Perkins, wife of one of Dad's fellow hunting buddies to go along.

The following Friday night Mom dressed me in heavy denim, knee boots, and even tied an uncomfortable cotton Roy Rogers scarf around my head. Handing us food and coffee, she said in a stern voice, "Young lady, keep that scarf on, and watch for snakes!"

As our party walked toward White Meade Cliff, a favorite hunting spot about two miles from home, I walked tall in my boots, trying my best not to fall on wet grass and thick brush. An excited George Alan leaped ahead, dragging me with him. Dad was leading two dogs, Marie, one, and Vick, her husband, was leading two.

Six dogs, I thought. A perfect number for a good race.

We chose a clearing, and made camp. Vick and Dad turned the dogs loose, and Marie and I spread blankets, and made a fire.

It took awhile, but the dogs picked up the scent, and the chase was on. Dad, Vick, and Marie seemed to know every dog out there. They all seemed the same to me. Loud.

Dad, leaning over, as if he too, would like to join the race, shouted, "There's goes ol' Sadie; she's leadin' the pack!"

Vick, not to be outdone, yelled, "There's Sam! Boy, he's sure raw-hidin' that fox!"

I jumped up, pulled my headscarf a little tighter, spit in the fire, and yelled, "George Alan, you damned old bag of bones, you're supposed to be a champion. Quit laggin' behind!"

I just took a wild guess. I hadn't heard his name mentioned, so I figured he must be behind.

Dad turned to Vick, and in a voice trembling with pride, said, "I've got myself a real little foxhunter here. I thought that since

I didn't have any sons, the family tradition wouldn't be carried on. Thank God I was wrong."

The night wore on, and I'd yell every chance I had, always for George Alan. "Boy, he's sure settin' the woods on fire!"

And he was.

Dad was thrilled.

"Cost me $40.00, but he's worth every dime of it," he said to me. "I spent the money I'd saved to buy a hog, and I thought your mother was going to run me off."

She said, "Spent our hog money, did you? I guess we'll just be without meat this winter."

I asked her, "Who in the hell ever heard of a hog chasin' a fox?"

I curled up beside him and must have slept, because the next thing I knew, he had me on his back carrying me out of the hollow.

We trudged home, happy hunters, and Mom met us at the door, relieved to see that her daughter still had her head scarf tied. She had prepared a delicious meal, and as we sat around the table, I was praised to the skies. Dad said that I could go hunting with them whenever I wanted.

Mom said, "Oh no, mister. Our daughter can go hunting when *I* want her to."

It was a good thing Mom didn't see those three kicks I received underneath the table, or breakfast would have been cancelled.

Dad's little foxhunter—me

Dad with his prized hound dogs
And a young Nadine looks on—1944

The Poorhouse

We sat in the middle of our large feather bed listening to the yelling as it ricocheted off walls and bounced upstairs to our room. Our parents' verbal fighting was as expected as our old rooster's crowing, his way of greeting a new day versus theirs.

"Do you think we'll live there?" whispered six-year-old Frankie.

"Gosh, I hope not," I answered.

"Where is it, anyway?" Frankie commented.

She thought I was a walking encyclopedia because I was three years older. Normally her questions annoyed me, but not this time.

I chewed on my long blonde hair as I answered, "The song says 'over the hill.'"

Mom and Dad's vicious arguments were always about money, or the lack of it. Dad was obsessed with money, and he drilled my poor mother relentlessly about how she should handle it. We heard him tell her over and over, "I get just as much pleasure from saving a dollar as you do from spending one."

"You got that right," she would retaliate. "*One* is all I'm allowed to spend."

As Dad left for work, slamming the door behind him, Frankie and I mouthed his parting words, "We'll end up in the poorhouse. Just wait and see!"

Prompted by the song, "Just Over the Hill to the Poorhouse," my sister and I set out to search for this deplorable place. Our house, surrounded as it was by hills, afforded us ample opportunity.

We spent afternoons climbing atop hills and looking over. We imagined this much-talked about house to be weathered, enveloped in thick fog, and filled with hungry people peering through barred windows.

We never found it, and we dared not question our parents for fear they'd take us before the appointed time. Dad was still threatening. Every morning.

My neurotic conviction concerning the poorhouse caused me to worry constantly about money. Our future, Frankie's and mine, was doomed. I guessed he'd already signed us over to the poorhouse, and we'd be placed there as soon as two inhabitants died.

I tried to postpone the inevitable by saving money. While participating in Sunday School Penny March, I held tightly to my penny. I didn't drop it in the plate. And I didn't spend my daily allowance. I saved every penny.

Dad's sister Opal took Frankie and me to church every Sunday morning. Mom and Dad did not attend, but saw to it that we did.

As I sat beside Aunt Opal after the customarily spoken prayer requests, Preacher Carl Robinson asked, "Will those in need please raise their right hand? God hears unspoken requests too."

Boy, was I in need! Frankie and I were headed to the poorhouse. With gusto, I raised my right hand. Aunt Opal pulled down my left one.

After the services as we walked to her car, Aunt Opal asked, "Hazel, what in the world made you raise your hands in prayer? You're only nine years old. I'm glad you believe in God answering prayer, but a child shouldn't be that troubled. What's bothering you?"

"Dad's sending me and Hazel to the poorhouse!" Frankie declared.

Aunt Opal had been holding Frankie's hand, and she dropped it and pulled Frankie around to face her.

"What's your dad been telling you girls?" she asked.

"We hear him and Mom every morning, and he keeps telling her we'll end up in the poorhouse," Frankie answered, her lower lip quivering.

Aunt Opal turned to me. "Is this true?"

"We looked all over the place and couldn't find it, but Dad says he's sending us. You know there's a song about it," I babbled.

"Get in the car girls!"

I'd never seen Aunt Opal so mad as when she confronted her brother a few minutes later. She didn't get through the front door before she began, "You ought to be horsewhipped, and if our daddy was alive he'd do it! You've scared these little girls half to death, threatening to end up in the poorhouse. If there was such a place, you should be made to live there!"

She said a lot more things I don't think she'd want Preacher Carl to hear, but she had Dad begging her to forgive him. He pulled us up on his lap, and told us not to worry. He said he loved us better than anything, and he'd never send us away—Mom, maybe, but not us. Frankie tuned up to cry, so he said he'd keep Mom too.

We heard a loud harrumph from the corner where Mom stood!

After that, things were peaceful—for two or three days. The rooster had no competition. His early-morning crowing was the only sound disturbing our sleep. Then Dad stumbled across Mom's Sears charge account. "You can wear your fancy dress to the poor-house!" he bellowed.

"I'd rather wear it to your funeral, you mink-eyed devil!" Mom screeched.

I was the last to leave home. I just couldn't leave, knowing I'd never find that kind of excitement any place else. I stayed with Mom and Dad until I turned 28. During that time, the rooster died, Frankie graduated from Radford College, and then married.

I worked full time as office manager for an auto parts store, purchased a '66 Ford Mustang convertible and enjoyed single life. Also, I was sole referee at home.

And there were plenty of rounds to referee. It took only trivial things such as "Avon calling" to get one under way. One day Mom's Avon lady, Lethia Justice, heard what Frankie and I knew by heart. "We'll end up in the poorhouse! Wasting good money I tell you!"

Mom whipped out her checkbook, wrote Lethia a check and told Dad, "Oh, shut up! We've lived in the poorhouse for years. Only we're situated *on* a hill, not *over* one!"

Cowgirls in Hog Heaven

Imagine a small wooden building complete with curtains, dolls, rocking chairs and numerous other toys.

Sound like a child's playhouse? It was. Typical? Not quite . . . this one was in the middle of a hog lot!

My friend Margaret, my sister, Frankie, and I made playhouses everywhere—in our basement, in Marg's basement and garage and our barn loft.

You name it and our playhouse had been there. Now we were looking for a new location . . . some place more *exciting*.

Every year, Dad kept two hogs, feeding them well during the summer to butcher in late fall. That summer of 1955, there was a black one and a red one. It was Frankie's and my job to feed them each evening, and if Marg was at our house, she usually helped.

They were kept some distance below the house in a large lot. In the center of the lot was a wooden building that had once been a chicken house.

"Bet I could have a playhouse there," I remarked one evening. "Red and Blackie wouldn't bother me at all."

"Bet you couldn't," Frankie and Marg challenged.

Never one to refuse a bet, I began moving my toys in the next day. The hogs just looked at me—I think they even welcomed my company. Soon I had a really nice playhouse, and Frankie and Marg wished it had been their idea instead of mine.

Playing Cowboys and Indians (or in our case, *Cowgirls* and Indians) was a favorite game with kids then. As the days passed,

Red and Blackie began to take on the appearance of cattle in our eyes.

We girls donned our Dale Evans straw hats and tied them under our chins, then proceeded to "round up" our "herd." In the heat of the day, we ran those hogs sometimes for half an hour at a time.

Dad couldn't understand it. I remember him talking to customers in his barbershop and asking Uncle Will Taylor, "You having any trouble with your hogs?"

Uncle Will answered, "Reckon not . . . only thing, the feed's so doggone high."

"You know," Dad would say, "I've fed those hogs more than any I've ever owned, and they keep *losing* weight."

For me, this went in one ear and out the other. I never realized it was because we were running Dad's hogs. I only knew we had the best playhouse ever, and it was such fun to live on a "ranch"!

The fun ended one day when Dad came home early and caught us chasing the hogs. We didn't understand his anger, but Marg didn't wait around for an explanation—she jumped the fence and ran for home! Frankie and I weren't so lucky.

Dad pulled us through the gate and marched us home. All the way up the road, I begged and promised I'd never do it again. After all, the hogs were having fun, weren't they?

Dad had words for Mom when we got to the house. "How could you let them *do* this, Effie?" he demanded.

"I had no idea," Mom countered. "I thought they were playing in the barn loft."

"Well, maybe it was better they weren't in the loft," Dad said. "They'd probably set fire to the hay!"

Later that fall, the hogs were butchered. Afterward, Dad saw how upset I was and sat me on his lap.

"Honey, this is the natural order of things," he explained. "Those hogs provide meat for us. You're not supposed to feel the way you do."

But that *was* the way I felt. I didn't eat meat for weeks—in fact, not until Christmas Day. Then no one, including me, could resist Mom's baked ham.

It was after Christmas dinner that I heard Dad remark, "You know, Effie, these are the leanest hams we've ever had. Maybe I'll let the kids chase the hogs again next summer . . ."

Mom, Frankie and me—1952

39

Monkey Shines

Bright-eyed, bushy-tailed and mean, that was Jo-Jo, the monkey. He belonged to my Aunt Bess Combs, who lived in Mt. Vernon, Ohio.

When I was nine years old, Mom, Dad, my younger sister, Frankie and I became friends with Jo-Jo.

It didn't start out that way though. Here's how it happened.

My dad never owned a vehicle during our "growing up" years, so Frankie and I had never been away from home except for occasional short bus trips to neighboring towns. When we were invited to visit in Ohio, imagine our excitement. Uncle Ruey May would drive down for us.

Frankie and I planned for days in advance. We dressed our dolls in their finest clothes and had them ready to take with us. We spent hours building a box in which to transport two hound pups. They were only six weeks old and we couldn't leave them home! Needless to say, we were disappointed in both ventures when Mom said a very definite, "NO!"

Finally, the big day arrived! Frankie and I sat in the back, and each one had a window seat. Our faces were pressed to the glass; scared we'd miss something. I don't think we moved from the time we left home until we arrived in Ohio. Everything fascinated us. When we saw the Ohio River, we thought we'd reached the end of the earth. We craned our necks as we crossed it until we very nearly had whiplash.

When we reached our destination, Uncle Earlie met us at the car and helped carry in luggage. Aunt Bess and Cousin Betty hurried from the kitchen. As we hugged, we heard a whoop, and turned to find a monkey perched on the drapes. He chattered loudly as he swooped down to get in on the introduction too. My first impression of Jo-Jo was that he looked like Aunt Bess! Aunt Bess was small and lively, so was Jo-Jo. However, Jo-Jo owned a long tail and was an accomplished acrobat. I had yet to see Aunt Bess swing from drapes.

Dad and Mom eyed the monkey in an apprehensive way. Dad opened his mouth as if to say something. Mom raised her eyebrows at him, glanced at Jo-Jo and gave her head a tiny shake.

That evening, seated at the dinner table, Dad's misgivings turned to downright anger when Jo-Jo swung by and grabbed a dinner roll from him. Dad demanded, "Keep that dirty little thing away from me!"

Jo-Jo, happily munching on the roll, ignored all the commotion.

The next morning a little beady-eyed visitor hitting us in the head with a balled-up fist awakened us. We jumped out of bed and had a great time chasing him around the room. He was so quick and dodged all our attempts to catch him. Aunt Bess' dog, Teddy, got in the act, and the noise we created could be heard all along the block.

Junior, our cousin, had stopped by, and was standing inside the door, laughing at all the action. He stopped laughing and started fussing when Jo-Jo swung by and grabbed his cap. There he was, perched on the chandelier, his favorite spot, wearing Junior's red cap and a go-to-heck expression on his face!

Later in the day we were in the basement with Betty. Aunt Bess was a meticulous housekeeper, and had a place for everything. Her basement was cleaner than most people's living quarters.

A week before she had painted the basement stairs and stair railing white and for once, something was out of place. A gallon of red paint had been left setting on the gleaming white stairs.

Jo-Jo must have been bored with the color scheme and decided that now would be a good time to change it. He knocked over the can of paint, the lid dislodged, and red paint went everywhere!

Teddy's yelping brought Aunt Bess out of the kitchen. She looked down the basement steps, and began screeching at the top of her lungs.

Betty was yelling, "It's not my fault. If you hadn't gotten that monkey!"

Jo-Jo ran through the paint, coated his long tail, and was leaving a trail of red paint behind him. Teddy decided he was being ignored, so he made a lap or two through the paint.

Frankie and I dived into a corner and sat there until Aunt Bess stopped screeching, Betty dropped her voice an octave, Jo-Jo stopped running, and Teddy felt he didn't like all the attention after all.

The following morning Frankie and I helped stash luggage for our return trip home. Aunt Bess, Uncle Earlie and Betty waved us out of sight. Our eyes never left the little brown monkey perched on Aunt Bess' shoulder.

On the drive back to Virginia, Frankie and I talked about Jo-Jo until Dad threatened to put us out of Uncle Ruey's car. We begged and begged for a monkey; we cried, tried every tactic.

"Oh, Mom!" Frankie said over and over.

"P-l-e-a-s-e," I begged.

Finally Mom promised if we would just be quiet, she'd see that we got a monkey for Christmas.

We couldn't wait to tell our friends about the great time we'd had and about the things we'd seen and done. Top billing, of course, went to Jo-Jo, and to think, we gushed, "We'll have one just like him for Christmas. Mom promised!"

The following weeks we pestered Dad to build a cage for our promised monkey. He obliged. Frankie and I found leftover paint and scraps of linoleum. We spent happy hours painting the cage and placing linoleum on its floor. We wanted everything flawless for Jo-Jo, Jr.

We'd found the perfect spider monkey in *Sears Christmas Catalog*. We carried this catalog to neighbor's houses and proudly pointed him out to envious friends. We promised a party to celebrate his Christmas arrival.

Even now, it grieves me to think of that Christmas morning we kept listening for monkey sounds. We had the shining cage magnificently displayed under the tree with twinkling tinsel hanging from its roof. We sat there waiting for gifts to be handed out. But we couldn't hear or see a thing that *even resembled a monkey*.

Mom, Dad, Granny Combs and older sister, Nadine seemed uneasy and kept exchanging glances.

Granny said, "Now, children, sometimes we just don't get everything we want."

It didn't register what she could have meant, and I said, "Hurry up!"

Nadine handed a package to me and one to Frankie. Mom and Dad kept silent as we opened our gifts. Mine was a sock monkey, a stuffed gray and red wool sock, the heel making a perfect mouth and buttons sewn on to form his face. Frankie's was a little shaggy, brown, stuffed monkey with a set in plastic face and felt hands and feet.

Talk about monkeyshines — nothing Jo-Jo did could equal the one pitched by Frankie and me when we realized there would be no real-life monkey for us, only stuffed ones!

Eventually we loved those monkeys. We named them Bo-Bo and Jo-Jo. Bo-Bo the sock monkey was destroyed years ago; we completely trashed him though play.

However, Jo-Jo, minus a foot and hand, has retired to Frankie's attic. He resides there, surrounded by dolls, tea sets, picture albums, and other precious childhood memories, including a faded white homemade monkey cage.

He's in good company.

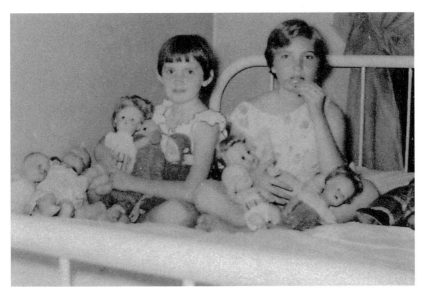

Frankie and me surrounded by toys — mid 1950s

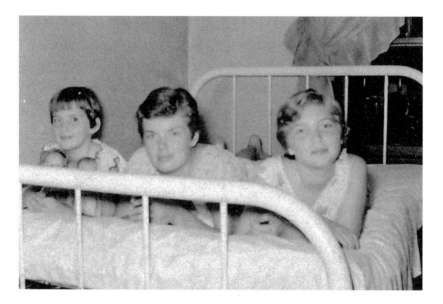

Frankie, Nadine and me

Uptown Girl

1363 Congress Street, Washington, D.C. No zip code

It was cold, snowing, and I had walked a mile to the post office before heading home from school. But holding Nadine's letter made me feel warm. I wanted to stop in Joe and Ruth Ball's grocery store to read it, but I knew Mom wouldn't like it. She enjoyed nothing more than having the family gather 'round while she shared Nadine's letter. As I trudged through the falling snow, I just didn't think I could stand the anticipation.

I cut across the now-empty schoolyard and on past Harvey Miller's toward home. Once there, I bounded up the twelve ice-covered cement steps, and in my haste, bumped into Granny Combs as she laboriously carried a filled coal bucket. We had no handrails, so she rocked from side to side and somehow managed to stay afoot and not drop the bucket.

"What's wrong with you, Hazel? Slow Down! You come a one causing me to fall and roll down all these slick steps."

"We got a letter from Nadine!"

Granny's frown was replaced by a bright smile.

"Well, what are we waiting for? Let's hurry on in the house."

"Ah, Granny, we'll just have to wait for Dad."

"Well, you know how he is. His feelings *would* be hurt."

I opened the door for Granny, and the heat from our Warm Morning coal-fed stove felt good as I pulled off my soggy woolen scarf, gloves, and snow-splattered coat. I hung them by the door and dashed to the kitchen. I found Mom lifting an iron skillet of corn bread from the big oven of her cook stove. As she flipped it onto a large plate, she asked why I was late coming home from school.

I pulled Nadine's letter from behind my back, and Mom's tired face broke into a wide smile.

She exclaimed, "You walked to the post office in this snow storm! I'm surprised school wasn't dismissed. Here sit by the stove and warm yourself while I take up supper. Your daddy should be home soon, and then we'll read Nadine's letter."

"Mom," she called to Granny Combs, "tell Frankie to come downstairs!"

Granny laid aside her sewing and walked to the stairs. She had inspected my coat and found a button missing. Never one to "put off tomorrow what should be done today," she immediately set about replacing the button.

Frankie had been upstairs cutting paper dolls, but when Granny told her a letter from Nadine had arrived, she ran down the stairs and wanted Mom to open it.

"I'll bet there's money for me and Hazel," Frankie said as she looked longingly at the letter.

"Well, we'll just wait until your daddy gets home. He'll be so tired from working in that awful mine, this will really make him feel better."

Frankie and I set the table, making plans for the money we fervently hoped was in the letter.

"Did it feel heavy?" Frankie asked as she carried food from the kitchen to the dining room.

I pinched off a piece of corn bread before answering, "I don't know, but I hope she remembers that we need spending money. It's embarrassing to take eggs to the store and trade them the way we did when we were kids. Well, for me anyway. You're still a kid. Artie Rickman is about the only one left who lets us do this."

"Yeah, I know," Frankie answered as she swiped a finger through mashed potatoes. "And don't call me kid!"

Mom, Granny, Frankie, and I thought Dad would never get home. He came through the door covered in coal dust and snow flakes.

"Boy! That old stove sure feels good. Gonna be a bad night. I hope you girls helped get in coal and kindling."

Granny poked her head around the door from the kitchen and assured Dad, "I have it all behind the stoves. Now, get in here, get cleaned up, and eat your supper! We got a letter from Nadine today."

Following our evening meal, Dad settled into his favorite old rocking chair. He sipped steaming coffee and nodded to Mom. Mom sat in a corner facing us and adjusted her glasses. Clearing her throat, she began reading.

Nadine's letters always began, "Hi folks." And ended: "all my love."

Between "hi folks" and "all my love," her letters were filled with excitement. Today, Mom read about her work at the Federal Bureau of Investigation. She had received a promotion from file clerk to that of a more responsible position—supervisor of her unit. Mom read that the promotion was based upon Nadine's excellence in leadership qualities.

At this point, Dad cleared his throat and Mom removed her glasses. She told us, "Mary Virginia Fletcher can be thanked for this. Miss Fletcher sort of took Nadine under her wing—all that 4-H work—those trips to Richmond . . . "

Granny commented from her corner of the room, "She's a Combs if I ever saw one."

Dad looked hard at Granny before saying, "Well, Adie, I reckon I didn't have a damn thing to do with gettin' her here, now did I?"

Flustered, Mom shook the pretty stationery. These had pictures of a snow-covered White House.

"Now, you two," Mom said, "let me finish."

Frankie and I never talked while Mom read Nadine's letters. We were afraid we'd miss something. Nadine had written to ask if it was OK to bring a roommate home for the holidays. Her name was Nina, and she was a Colorado native. Nadine had visited her some months before, and now she wanted to bring Nina to Southwest Virginia. Nina's parents were in Europe, and Nadine didn't want her to be alone at Christmas.

There was no money for Frankie and me, but the excitement of having Nadine and her friend home for Christmas helped soothe our disappointment.

The following weeks were filled with nonstop activity. Mom and Granny Combs cooked, cleaned, and spread the word that Nadine was coming home and bringing a rich friend. Frankie and I helped. At ages eleven and eight, we could paste wax linoleum floors, and clean varnished wood and French doors with Spic and Span water.

That Christmas was wonderful. Nadine brought a record player for Frankie and me, complete with a stack of popular records. Mom and Dad gave us board games, paper dolls, and books. Nina loved us, and we loved her. She was a beautiful girl — coal black hair, olive skin, and dark eyes. She brought gifts for all.

Dad was a little uncomfortable because he had to be on his best behavior. "Just wouldn't be right," he said, "seeing as how Nadine had company and all, for me to enjoy a little liquid Christmas cheer."

Nadine loved city living. I believe those were her happiest days. Shortly after this visit, she and J. B. Crabtree, a hometown guy, began dating. Three years later they married, and she returned home. She was restless then, and she still is. She wouldn't trade her family for anything. She supported school events involving her children, and for years our entire family celebrated Christmas with Nadine, J. B., son Mark, and daughter, Michele. Their home was our home.

She travels. I believe it's an escape form the boredom of small town life that she's explored every state in the nation, Ireland, Mexico, and the Bahamas.

She never complains, but even after all these years she'll bring up an adventure from those uptown-girl days.

Nadine

J.B. and Nadine's children, Mark and Michele—Christmas 1966

Bells and Barn Lofts

Spring! Glorious spring! And here I am imprisoned in a stuffy old classroom. I close my eyes and smell the freshly plowed ground; can almost feel the dirt between my bare toes. These black and white saddle oxfords are killing me, especially worn with bobby sox. Why can't I skip school once in a while, like one day a week? Besides, I need a break to read all those Zane Grey westerns. Between chores and studying, there's little time for reading.

Walking home from school, these questions dance through my mind. However, being the brilliant strategist I am, I soon find a solution to my problem.

Our house is located within walking distance of the Swords Creek Elementary School. In fact, only a fence separates Dad's property and the school's playground.

Dad complains about the bells; says they frighten his horses.

Each morning three bells ring. Two warning bells, and a third announcing class time. Always, I'm inside the building on the first bell.

As my mind continues working overtime, I decide to make bold changes. First, I'll take blankets, a pillow and my cherished westerns to the barn loft. Next, I'll begin saving my recess money. I can easily skip a few Brown Mules. Finally, I won't leave home until the first bell sounds.

Once my plans are laid, a week passes quickly and I'm ready. I don't leave home until I hear the first school bell. Instead of waking across the playground as I usually do, I walk the opposite direction to Rickman's Grocery located near the school. With my week's savings, I buy a Nehi Orange soda, a moon pie and a bag of chips. The third bell finds me cutting across a vacant lot towards Dad's barn.

I carefully screen the area. I'm safe from my parents because Dad has been in the fields for hours, and Mom is seated at the kitchen table enjoying her second cup of perked Standard coffee. No neighbors in sight, so I slip around the side of the chestnut wood, tin-roofed barn. Easing the door open, I walk across the hay strewn manger to the stairs leading to the loft.

It's cool there so I snuggle in the blankets and sleep. The ringing of the morning recess bell wakes me. The warm sun now shining through the cracks in the loft's boards creates a stripped floor pattern. I count them, reveling in my freedom. I throw the blanket aside, rearrange my pillow and reach for *Under the Tonto Rim*. I become so engrossed in reading when I hear the lunch bell sound, I'm amazed at how fast time flies. I eat my delicious lunch. I read two more chapters, but the cozy warmth of the sun and food make me drowsy. I wake to the sound of the afternoon recess bell. I prepare to leave the loft, and the first dismissal bell finds me walking across the field towards school.

The third bell finds me walking from school and back across the same field with my sister as I do each afternoon when school is dismissed.

Once a week I take a break from school and read a total of ten books. As report card time draws near, between thoughts of "This is living!" and "Freedom, glorious freedom!" a nagging troubling thought intrudes. How in the world can I explain all these days marked absent? Dare I try to erase them? Mom and Dad will 'wear the hide' off me. I have to do something.

As I climb the stairs leading to my loft—I'm now claiming it as mine—I throw off these sobering thoughts. It's a gorgeous

May day, and soon I'll be riding the range with a handsome cowboy.

I'm well into *Twin Sombreros* when I feel I'm no longer alone. Someone or something is watching me. I look all around, see nothing, so I resume reading. The feeling persists. I lean back to straighten my pillow and almost faint. Wrapped around a rafter directly above my head is the largest snake I've ever seen! His beady eyes are glassy and his forked tongue is doing a tango.

I don't hesitate. I bolt for the door, and jump from the loft. The hay stacked beneath the door cushions my fall and prevents injury. Shaking, screaming, and deathly pale, I run home and through the door, giving my poor mom a terrible fright.

After calming down a bit, I confess everything. To my surprise, Mom laughs. She even hugs me!

She says, "Young lady, don't think for a minute I approve of what you've done. But, it's like seeing my life relived through you."

She continues to explain that as a youth she had done similar things. She loved to read, and was called a dreamer by her family and friends.

After our enlightening conversation, Mom goes to the loft, retrieves my hide-away treasures, and walks with me to school. She promises to talk with my seventh grade teacher, and not tell Dad—this time.

Realizing how I'm dreading entering the classroom during mid-day, she embraces me, and says in a soothing voice, "I'm right beside you, and I'll see that no punishment awaits you. I think your encounter with Mr. Blacksnake was punishment enough."

Mom, Dad and "Old Maude" — 1956

Frankie, me and Patricia Rickman Lambert — 1956

A Few Kind Words

That hog's hide must have been tough as leather, I thought, as I helped Mom push and shove the heavy Warm Morning stove across the linoleum-covered floor. We had carefully placed meat skins, greasy side down, underneath the stove and were now halfway across the living room. Our destination, the back porch, was two rooms away.

When the weather became warm enough to no longer need a fire in the coal-and-wood-burning heater, the ritual of removing the stove began. The stove's removal was eagerly anticipated because it eliminated two things: a few of the harsher outside chores and the mess created in the house from coal/wood smoke and scattered ashes. I hated carrying in heavy loads of wood, but even more, emptying ashes. Usually, ashes were scattered over a garden site, and it meant walking a good distance from the house. This was especially rough in bitter cold mountain weather, but it wasn't a fun thing to do at any time.

The changing season also meant another ritual, spring cleaning.

After Mom and I finally maneuvered the stove through the house and onto the porch, Mom set about initiating this second ritual. "Hazel, bring the Spic and Span, and that box of Tide washing powders. Get them old rags from under the kitchen cabinet."

I carried these things to Mom who was standing on a rickety wooden table. She was busy wiping soot tags from the living room wall.

"Mom, be careful! That thing could rear up with you," I cautioned as I placed her cleaning supplies near by.

"Oh, I know how close to the edge to get," she said. "I need this wall washed down, so while I work, you and Frankie take your wagon up to the Goodman's and play with Judy and David. Tomorrow, if it's a sunny day, we'll tear down the bedsteads and drag the mattresses and springs outside. Ah, there's nothing like a good clean house."

I left her singing and working as I went in search of my eight-year-old sister, Frankie.

I found her playing with dolls. I asked, "Wonder why they call them bedsteads? Maybe it's 'cause they sleep like a rock 'stead of a bed!"

Frankie didn't understand my attempt at humor, and kept on combing her doll's hair. Just as I was about to ask if she wanted to ride wagons with Judy and David, we heard a loud crash accompanied by an even louder scream.

I grabbed Frankie's hand and we dashed in the house. There lay Mom sprawled on the floor covered in soapsuds and dirty water. The equally dirty rag looked as if it had been placed over a dead person's face. Her water-splattered glasses had been thrown across the floor. The wobbly little table was lying on its top, its four legs like arms raised in victory.

Scared silly, Frankie and I stared at Mom. I stood there holding Frankie's hand. She squeezed my hand until it grew numb.

"Children," Mom finally moaned, "run get Stella!"

"Stay here with Mom!" I said to Frankie. "I'll be right back."

"No! I'm coming with you," a frightened Frankie answered, and clutching her doll, ran with me.

Our neighbor, Stella Stiltner was in her vegetable garden. Breathless, we told her about Mom. She'd been busy preparing a lettuce bed. Throwing her hoe in the air, barely missing us, she broke into a run. We followed.

Bursting through the door, we found Mom just as we'd left her. Clucking her tongue, Stella began, "Effie, I've told you not once, but a thousand times, you'll get hurt on that old table."

Mom groaned, and shook her head from side to side as she whispered, "Don't fuss at me, Stella. I know my leg is broken."

Stella went into action. She told us in a stern, no-back-talk-tone, "Don't leave your Mom! Hazel, get a cold cloth and bathe her face. Frankie, you're old enough to help clean this mess."

The closest telephone was in Artie Rickman's Grocery, located below our house, so Stella ran down the hill. She was gone for what seemed forever, but was barely fifteen minutes. She bent over Mom and stroked her hair back from her face. "Gent's ambulance is on the way, but I'm afraid you'll have to go as you are. I'm not about to move you."

Mom, a proud woman, could only cry, as much from humiliation as from pain. She crossed her arms and tried to cover up the ratty housedress.

Stella then said, "I called the mines and told Herman to bring Beach home."

Mom groaned louder.

Dad and the ambulance arrived at the same time. Coal dust clung to Dad, and his face was creased in a frown. Brows knit, eyes glaring and walking fast, all he needed was a set of horns to rival the devil himself. He slammed the door. He didn't bother to ask about Mom before yelling, "Don't you have any sense? I've told you to stay off that table!"

Why didn't you buy her a step ladder, I wanted to say, but knew better.

Stella, Frankie and I stood beside Mom as if our presence would protect her from Dad's anger.

"Beach, I'm hurt," Mom answered weakly.

"I'm going to burn that table," Dad continued as if Mom hadn't spoken.

Stella couldn't take it anymore. "Beach," she said as if speaking to a naughty child, "get yourself cleaned up, and have Herman drive you to the hospital. And when you get there, act like you have some sense!"

Dad, furious with Stella for talking down to him, and with Mom for having the nerve to ruin a day's pay, began pacing the floor.

Frankie and I had moved away from Mom and stood observing from our hiding place behind the bedroom door.

As the men carefully placed Mom on the gurney, we remained out of the way. We moved to a window and watched as she was just as carefully loaded into the ambulance. Neither of us moved until the ambulance was out of sight.

Frankie and I spent the afternoon with Stella. We kept asking questions about what would happen to Mom at the hospital.

A subdued Dad arrived home before dark and told us Mom had a compound fracture to her right leg. "Girls, I've got to work, so until Granny Combs gets here, you'll stay with Bertie Goodman."

Three days later our maternal grandmother, Ada (Granny) Combs was with us. The "Little General" soon had everything running smoothly. She even had Dad smiling, and kept him in a good mood by cooking his favorite foods.

Mom slowly healed, but during her lifetime, she suffered several more fractures.

A victim of osteoporosis, her life was riddled with pain. She smiled through this pain, and still managed household chores, sometimes with the aid of a walker.

Mom's growing dependence on Dad fueled his short temper. He'd grumble, "If I'm in the garden, I have to stop what I'm doing, go in the house and change the television channel."

The year my sisters and I gifted them with a new television, complete with remote control, Dad said the gadget with all the numbers was the greatest invention since Edison's light bulb.

In retrospect, I know Dad loved my mother. I only wish this mountain man had listened when Mom said on several occasions, "I don't want much. I'd settle for a few kind words."

Mom — recovering from hospital stay

My beautiful mother, Effie Combs (Hale) at age 20 — 1930

Oh! The Shame of It

"When you hear the word 'procto,' wrap your split-tail gown around you and head for the nearest swamp!" The late southern comedian Jerry Clower, must have borrowed these words from my Granny (Ada) Combs.

Granny, in spite of her outgoing personality, was modesty personified. She didn't fail to preach her beliefs to her granddaughters either. For instance, short-shorts headed her list of devil's tools. For Granny, other scandalous modes of dress included jeans and swimsuits. She was appalled when Nadine wore her cardigan as a pullover. She buttoned the sweater up the back, leaving enough buttons to form a V, thereby exposing some skin.

Granny said to Mom, "No daughter of mine ever left the house dressed that way. What's this world coming to?"

Granny's world was shaken to the core due to an experience in her doctor's office. She had been moping around for days, complaining of first one thing, then another. Finally, after much persuading on Mom's part, Granny agreed to see her physician, Doctor J. A. Robinson.

The day of her appointment arrived, and Mom was unable to accompany Granny to the doctor's office. So, I was allowed to miss a day of school to be with her. We rode the C. C. Self bus to Richlands to the Clinch Valley Clinic Hospital.

While we were in the waiting room area, Granny became figidity; she didn't like hospitals or doctors. Finally, she was called in to see her doctor.

When she emerged from the office some thirty minutes later, she was again her old cheerful self. She said, "Well, I'm to come back next week for what he called a 'procto.' There must not be much to it; Dr. Robinson didn't seem all that concerned."

Of course, I had no idea what a procto was, so I answered with an enthusiastic "Good!" I was just happy to see Granny happy.

The following weeks were not rose-colored ones at our house. The *medicine* Dr. Robinson had prescribed for Granny was, in fact, high-powered laxatives. Granny, being unable to read labels was in a total state of confusion. She could not understand why she had to be put through such misery for just a procto.

Frankie and I, bursting with curiosity, questioned Mom, endlessly. "Mom, what is a procto? Will it hurt? Will Granny have to stay in the hospital? Don't you think she's losing weight?"

Mom answered, "You don't need to know, and for goodness sake, just don't mention it to your Granny!"

No need to worry. We couldn't mention anything to Granny. It wasn't easy catching her to and from her many trips to the bathroom.

Once again, I accompanied Granny back to the hospital. It was a pleasant spring morning, and Granny said it might be wise to leave a little earlier than usual to await the 11:00 a.m. bus. She was, for some strange reason, feeling weak and dizzy, so she would need to move slower. While we walked down the hill, several neighbors waved and called greetings to Granny, so by the time we reached the bottom of the hill, the bus was already in sight.

Suddenly, Granny turned to me and exclaimed, "Lord, have mercy! I forgot my bloomers! You run back to the house and get them. I'll tell the driver I left our bus fare and sent you for it."

I ran up the hill as fast as my ten-year-old legs could go. After all, I had the all-important task of delivering Granny's bloomers.

Returning, I bounced up the bus steps and shyly handed Granny her bloomers. She was busy talking and laughing to the driver, and never missing a beat, she slipped her underwear inside her handbag. I eased into the seat beside her and quickly turned my head toward the window. The shame of it!

For Granny, the "shame of it" lay just ahead. Sitting in the same seat I had occupied the week before, I heard strange sounds coming from Dr. Robinson's office. Granny had been called some minutes earlier, and as she started for the office, she cheerfully said to me, "Don't worry. I'll be right back."

"Right back" stretched into long minutes, a half-hour, and finally an entire hour passed. All the while, I could hear Granny's raised voice, first screaming, then crying. I could also hear the nurse talking in soothing tones, trying to settle Granny down.

Granny had been in there for so long, I was afraid we'd miss the bus. Finally, she came out looking not at all the way Granny should look. Her glasses weren't sitting straight, her carefully twisted bun of hair was on the opposite side of her head to where it should be, the seams in her black silk stockings were crooked, and her dress was crumpled as was her face. What had they done to Granny to make her cry?

On the ride back to Swords Creek, she said not a word. When I'd try to talk to her, she'd just pull her lace-edged handkerchief from her handbag and wipe her eyes.

When Granny and I arrived home, Mom immediately saw Granny was terribly upset. "Go to your room, Hazel," she gently said. I slipped up to the landing on the stairs and stopped. I needed to know what this was all about.

Granny moaned, "Effie, how *could* you send me up there knowing what they would do to me? I'll never be able to face that doctor again. I'll never be able to walk down the street without dropping my head in shame. Lord, have mercy on me! I'm going to pack my bags, leave here, and if I ever hear the word procto again, I'll just keep on going!"

Sitting on the stairs' landing, straining my ears, I heard a lot of talk, but no explanations. Why did Granny feel this way? Just because she forgot her bloomers was no reason to leave home!

The next morning, sure enough, Granny carried her cardboard suitcase down the hill. I trudged along beside her, feeling very downhearted. I always missed her when she was away, and I told Granny this as I stood with her, waiting for the bus. I helped with her luggage as she climbed aboard. A forlorn little figure she made as she sat there, clutching her black patent leather handbag to her breast.

I stood there in the bright April sunshine waving her out of sight, thinking, Granny, I sure hope you remembered your bloomers. I can't chase that bus all the way into the state of Ohio!

Granny with grandsons Jim and John May. Howard, Ohio—1950

Frankie, Mom and me

Remembering Our Early Years

Barber Shop Saturday Mornings

During the 1950s and 1960s, Saturday mornings were always busy at our house because this particular day was Dad's "hair cuttin' day." Dad was a self-taught barber, and set up shop right in the house. Looking back, it's a wonder we, including Dad, survived it all.

Not only did he barber, but he was a coal miner, farmer, and fox hunter. He worked in a mine during winter months, farmed during summer months, raised/sold fox hounds, and hunted year 'round.

A typical Saturday morning began with the 'phone ringing, and someone asking, "Is Beach cuttin' hair today?" Then, men and boys began arriving. If it was during summer months, the front porch and steps soon filled.

Dad's barber chair, a home-made wooden stool with a cane bottom was placed in the center of the porch directly below the porch light. I've known him to cut hair until way past dark. A leather strap hung from the right side on which Dad sharpened his straight razor. He kept his barber tools in a cardboard box, and one of my earliest memories is Mom telling me, "Don't you dare mess with your daddy's barber tools!" Of course I completely ignored this warning. I was fascinated with his electric clippers, and kept my arms shaved slick. Play time ended, however, when my first grade teacher, Sadie Ball, sent Mom a note asking why Hazel had such coarse hair growing on her arms.

I loved watching Dad cut hair, and even more I wanted to be around all the excitement and commotion. When cold weather brought the shop back inside from the porch, Mom and Granny Combs tried to keep Frankie and me upstairs in our rooms. I'd sit on the top step out of sight, and listen as the men discussed politics, mining, and hunting. What tales! I learned to "cuss" by the time I was a four-year-old, and because of it, felt several licks from Dad's leather strap.

I especially liked it when Garnett Ray was there. He could really "pour it on" Dad. For example, he'd say, "Beach, you old tight wad. You might not go to hell for a dollar, but you'd play around the edges and fall in!"

Dad answered, "You long-necked s.o.b., at least if I swallowed a green apple, it wouldn't be ripe by the time it reached my stomach!"

Come to think of it, Garnett didn't pull much on Dad.

There was *always* lively conversation at the barber shop. I remember once when Frank Vance and Hobert Miller were there. Now, Hobert (Hobe) preached some, and Frank wasn't known for attending church. Dad had Hobe in the barber chair when suddenly Hobe thought it might be a good time to deliver a sermon to Frank. He began: "Mr. Vance, if you don't get to church, the devil is going to reach right up through the ground, and get you."

Frank didn't take to this, and he answered, "Hobe Miller, he'll get you before he does me!"

Not to be outdone, Hobe squinted his left eye, looked hard at Frank, and said, "By gum, buddy, if he does, he'll get me on my knees!"

This time Dad laid down his tools and laughed as Frank stomped out of the house. Frank later came back, and said he was through with Hobe Miller!

By the time I reached 16, I wasn't all that enthused with Dad's barber business. I tried to arrange a date so that I could be at my sister Nadine's house when he came to call for me. I certainly wasn't ashamed of Mom and Dad, but it wasn't a good feeling to have someone be given the third degree by ten or fifteen men seated around the house.

I remember one particular Saturday the summer of 1962 because at the time of the incident, it seemed earth-shattering to me. Nadine, her husband, and infant son were out of town, so I had no choice but to have my date come to the house. Now, during the sixties, at least in Swords Creek, men just didn't wear shorts. When I looked out a window and saw my date walking towards the house wearing Bermuda shorts, I had a terrible feeling that he would always remember this day.

When he reached the house, Dad shut off his clippers, and the young man introduced himself. He extended his hand, but Dad was too busy looking at his legs to notice, and so were the men seated on the porch and steps. My date then asked Dad if he would please inform me that he was there.

Dad looked at him and said, "No, I won't because I don't want her scared to death!"

Then, Dad, along with everyone erupted into loud, boisterous laughter. My date was so astonished he walked off the porch, and out the yard. On his way to the car he heard remarks such as, "Just look at them legs! Don't they remind you of two ropes with knots tied in 'em!"

I was mortified, and didn't even try to contact him. I never saw him again.

Some years later, Dad moved his barber shop from our house to the small rental house he owned located directly below where we lived. Before, he refused to relinquish the rent money, but Mom made it so rough on him he reluctantly agreed to the change.

Once there, however, he was much better satisfied, and his business improved. Many men, out of respect for us, wouldn't come to the house. Also, the good times got better. Now, there was music. Frank Vance on the fiddle, Garnett Ray on the banjo, Bill Fields on the guitar, and all of them, Dad included, from time-to-time on the floor! Seems old Crow Whiskey had flown in with the music.

These people were all special to me. No, they weren't church-going people, at least not then, but they were fun-loving, warm-hearted people. I never heard them talking about their neighbors because they were too busy poking fun at each other. The only ones they hurt were themselves. *They* suffered hangovers.

I feel they weren't given enough credit for the good they did. Lots of little children ate better because of some of these men. I've been there when money was passed from the ones who had to the ones in need.

I remember them with fondness, and I feel blessed to have known them. Because of them, I learned at a very early age to look beyond outward appearances, and glimpse the real person within.

Frankie and me standing in front of Tommy and Eula Land's car
— Swords Creek, 1965

Spencer and me — 1978 (Spencer sporting a Beach Hale haircut)

Ralphster and the Rosebush

During the early 1960s it was considered a big event when someone living in Swords Creek purchased a new vehicle. He or she was the talk of the neighborhood for weeks.

Ralph Miller wanted to stretch his notoriety to months.

During June 1963, he purchased a new jeep. Ralph waxed the already shiny green vehicle until it became so slick, it was dangerous for a fly to land on it. He then rode up and down the Creek, making sure everyone saw it.

Ralph and his family lived in the holler just above us, and each time he passed our house, he'd sound the horn. Following a hard day's work, Dad enjoyed after supper coffee while seated on our front porch swing. As Ralph honked, at the same time each evening, Dad always laughed and remarked, "Well, I've seen Ralphster in his jeepster, so I guess I can go inside and watch Chet and David."

I took one unforgettable ride in the "jeepster." Ralph's daughter Nadine invited me to attend church services with them. By the time we arrived at church, and I had crawled from under the floor mat, I promised myself if I got back home alive, I'd never get in that jeep again. When I mercifully did get home, I told my family, "Ralph Miller drives like a mad man! He is really going to hurt someone, but that someone won't be me!"

My prophecy was fulfilled the following day. Ralph had his dad, "Uncle" Harvey, (when I was young, it was customary to address our elders as uncle or aunt), and his brother Lester in the jeep, and was traveling at his usual high rate of speed.

At the foot of the hill, there was a large drainpipe located on the left side of the dirt road. Hazel Cline, who lived there, was best known for her beautiful lawn, and immaculate house. In order to conceal the drainpipe, and beautify the area, Hazel had planted a wild rosebush. This rosebush had grown and spread until it covered the entire top of the pipe.

Ralph approached this turn-off to the road that led to his house without even slowing. In fact, he swung in there on two wheels, and flipped his jeep into the rosebush. All four wheels kept spinning like there was no tomorrow!

Lester, who had been riding comfortably in the back, with his elbows propped up on the back of Uncle Harvey's and Ralph's seats, couldn't understand why he was suddenly up-seated, and in a rosebush, of all places. He could smell the roses, but he could also feel the thorns!

Ralph crawled out of the driver's seat, scratched and scared. "I've killed Pap," he yelled. "I've killed Pap!"

Frankie had been riding her bike down the hill when Ralph met the rosebush. She was picking herself up from the side of the road where she'd wrecked.

Neighbors came running.

Artie Rickman, owner and operator of a grocery store directly across from the accident, had been standing on the store porch talking with Hazel Cline. After realizing no one was seriously injured, they laughed so hard they had to hold on to the porch rails for support!

Uncle Harvey had crawled out of the passenger side, shirt torn, glasses scratched, and his cap askew. He began limping up the hill toward home, refusing Artie's offer to drive him. "No thanks. I'll walk!"

And to Ralph he said, "Son, I'll never let you drive me again!"

To my knowledge he never did. Not in the jeep.

Frankie — 1962

Old Rose and Me

Will that darn dog ever shut up?, I wondered. She had been doing this same mournful howling routine for the past half-hour. Eleven p.m., but did she care? You bet your life she didn't! She was letting everyone within hearing distance know just how disappointed she was at being left behind. After all, she could chase a fox with the best of them!

It was the summer of 1966, and Dad had gone fox hunting as he usually did each weekend. Sometimes, he would take five or six dogs, and he and some of his fellow hunting buddies would leave Friday night. If it was a good chase, we wouldn't see him until late Sunday afternoon. Usually, he took all the dogs, just leaving the pups behind. This time, however, Rose suffered sore feet and had to be left behind too. She certainly didn't like it and was staging a one-dog, all-night protest.

I tossed and turned and tried putting a pillow over my head. I even put cotton in my ears. Nothing worked. In those days, we didn't have electronic gadgets as a means of distraction.

I stuck my head out my upstairs window, yelled everything imaginable at Rose, and she just howled louder. Finally, in desperation, I threw my shoes at her. I could have sworn I saw teeth flash in the moonlight. That dog was laughing at me!

It was now twelve a.m., and she showed no signs of slowing down. She had that imaginary fox on the run. Well, I wasn't about to listen to the entire race.

I got out of bed, grabbed Mom's broom on my way outdoors, and paid Rose a visit. In my anger, I hit her more than I should have. Animal cruelty sickens me, but Rose had pushed me too far.

After I returned to bed, I didn't hear a peep out of her. I called to her; she made no response. I worried that I had killed her, and prayed she'd begin howling again. She was Dad's favorite, and I knew I was in for it if I had hurt Rose. I fretted all night, but I was afraid to check on her.

Mom had just placed breakfast on the table and I prayed first that Rose was all right, and second that Dad wouldn't return home until Sunday. That would give me one more day. If Rose was still alive, maybe I could get her to a veterinarian. I hadn't even said "amen" when Dad came through the door.

He was usually so jolly when he returned from fox hunting. After all, he had the best dogs in Russell County, minus one, I thought. Why was he frowning? Oh mercy, did he find Rose dead? "Effie," he said to Mom, "did you hear anything at the dog lot last night?"

Mom looked at me, saw the pure agony on my face, and replied, "No, why do you ask?"

"Well," answered Dad, "there's lumps as big as hen eggs all over old Rose's head."

I couldn't stand it any longer. "Is she alive, Dad?"

"Yes, she's alive, but it looks like she's been in a fight with a bobcat."

"She's alive," was all I heard, and I felt so grateful, until I saw the look on my sister Frankie's face. You little devil, I thought, you'll hold this over my head until I'm walking on a cane.

I can't begin to mention how many times through the years I handed over my car keys, new clothes, paid her way into movies, you name it. All it took was "I remember old Rose."

I was thirty-five years old, and all the family had gathered home for Mother's Day, when the subject of Dad's dogs was brought up.

Frankie delighted in telling Dad the story of how I almost killed Rose. Dad did just what I knew he'd do—he became so furious he asked me to leave!

It bothered me, and I had a hard time sleeping that night. I was sitting in my bedroom, looking out on a moonlit lawn, when I saw something flash and heard a dog's gleeful yelp.

Darn that Rose, she was still laughing at me!

Déjà Vu

My uncle H. B. "Shorty" Strouth assumed his favorite back-seat position this hot 1968 July Saturday as he and long-suffering wife, Mary Wiggins (Wigg) prepared to drive to the hospital to bring my mother home.

Mom had been a patient at the Clinch Valley Clinic Hospital in Richlands for six days, and she had telephoned home this morning. "My doctor signed the release papers when he made his rounds, so you need come get me."

We didn't own a vehicle, and Dad hated to bother my sister Nadine who had her hands full with small children Mark and Michele. After pondering the situation, he decided to call his sister. Aunt Wigg said she'd be more than glad to drive up to nearby Richlands and bring Effie home.

That settled, Dad, Frankie, and I set about getting the house ready. We'd let the place go while Mom was away, and it was a mess. Dad and I worked full time at our jobs, and Frankie, who was a college student, had a summer job. Consequently, we had very little time at home, and besides, it was more fun to sit on our front porch in late evenings, sip coffee, and listen as Dad shared tall tales.

He'd begin, "You girls need to clean the house before your mother gets home, but we'll talk a while." Two hours later, we were still talking!

Mom had suffered a fall, broken her right leg again, and dislocated her right shoulder. This time tests were finally ordered (she'd complained for years about joint pain) and results revealed she had severe osteoporosis.

I had visited every day, and made sure Mom was treated well by hospital staff. She tried to appear brave, but I sensed her worry and concern, not so much for herself, but for Dad. Her first question, "How's your dad?"

I'd joke and get her laughing by telling her he'd lost several pounds due to my cooking, but other than that, he was OK. "He really misses you, Mom." I hastened to add. And he did.

And today she was coming home.

I could imagine the ride to the hospital, Uncle Shorty in the back seat directly behind Aunt Wigg. He'd always lean in with his elbows, one on each side of her head. He read every traffic sign from Swords Creek to Richlands. He'd caution, "Slow down, now Wiggie!"

Aunt Wigg chain-smoked and tried to ignore him.

Soon they were driving the circular drive leading to the hospital. After it was confirmed that Aunt Wigg and Uncle Shorty would bring Mom home, we'd called and the nurse relayed the message to Mom. There was no phone in Mom's room because Dad said he would not pay that ridiculous fee.

Mom had time to have her things packed, and she was in the lobby waiting as the new blue-and-white Chevy pulled up.

Aunt Wigg and Uncle Shorty stepped from the car, and Aunt Wigg stashed Mom's case in the trunk while Uncle Shorty held open the car's back door as attendants carefully helped Mom into the car.

Aunt Wigg maneuvered the front seat to allow Mom as much room as possible, and told Uncle Shorty, "Get up here with me!"

He strongly objected, and resumed his back seat navigator position.

She looked hard at her stubborn husband, but said nothing as she slid behind the driver's seat, and lit a cigarette. She put the car in gear, and began the descent off the hill. She slowed, prepared to stop at the bottom, but Uncle Shorty gave the command, "Go, Wiggie! Go! All Clear!"

Aunt Wigg drove straight into the path of an oncoming vehicle, and when their car stopped spinning, it was headed back up the hill! Mom was moaning in pain, and Uncle Shorty said over and over again, "Why didn't you look where you were going, Wiggie!"

"Wiggie" pushed her hair from her eyes, retrieved her burning Chesterfield cigarette from the floorboard, and picked up her oversized handbag. She calmly stepped from the car, and jerked Shorty from the back seat. She literally beat him black and blue with that handbag.

Mom, whose birth date was the same as Shorty's, felt a bond with this brother-in-law because he never failed to buy her a gift on their special day. Between moans, she begged Aunt Wigg, "Don't kill him!"

If Uncle Shorty had been wearing an odometer, it would have registered 50 miles. He was still making laps around the Chevy when the ambulance arrived. The investigating crash officer was enjoying the show!

Mom *and* Uncle Shorty were transported back up the hill. Aunt Wigg stayed with her car, and was issued a ticket for failing to yield right-of-way. Shorty was released, but kept insisting, "I hurt all over, and I'm not in good enough shape to go home."

The attending physician finally agreed that he could spend the night, and Uncle Shorty was smiling as they wheeled him toward the elevator. He knew he'd be safe, at least for the night.

Mom was taken back to her room, and while attendants were putting her to bed, the bed fell! Poor Mom. This fall damaged her back, and she was placed in a back brace. She now had a full plaster leg cast, a partial plaster shoulder cast, and a back brace.

Aunt Wigg's car suffered damage, but she could drive it.

Not yet knowing any of this, we were seated on the porch waiting to help get Mom in the house when Aunt Wigg pulled up. Of course, we realized something was wrong when we saw the car all smashed in front, and only one occupant.

Dad was the first to her, and we followed closely behind.

Aunt Wigg explained the situation.

"Well, I'll be @$&*! I don't blame you, sis. You should have done this a long time ago. Ever since you began church, you've let Shorty boss you around. I kept wondering when we'd see the old Wigg again. I've been ashamed of you! Hales just ain't made to take a bunch of crap, and I don't think the good Lord intends for us to be jerked around."

Mom spent two more weeks at the hospital. Shorty hitched a ride home next day, and lived to talk about it. Aunt Wigg's car was repaired, and when Mom was released from the hospital she again volunteered to bring her home, but this time she went alone.

When September 26 rolled around that year Uncle Shorty received a sympathy card from Mom along with the birthday card and gift she always gave.

Aunt Wigg, son Johnny, and sister Opal

Uncle Shorty, son Terry
(T.J.) and Aunt Wigg

Life Lessons Seen Through a Windshield

I stood by the side of the road silently cursing and wishing Margaret Rickman and Nadine Miller were on their way to Hades instead of Richlands. This was the second morning in a row they'd done me this way. I was even paying Margaret to ride with her. I was employed at Roydon's Clothing Store, and she and Nadine were employed at Ben Franklin 5 & 10.

Neither I nor my dad owned a vehicle. I couldn't even drive. I was puzzled and hurt because I hadn't done anything to cause them to behave this way.

I was frantic. How was I to get to my job? "One more day," my employer had warned me yesterday, "and you're gone." I was just standing by the roadside pondering what to do when Artie, Margaret's mother, came across the road. She had been watching from the window of her store, and she was furious with Margaret.

She said, "Hazel, I'll close the store and drive you to work."

"Thanks, Artie, but I have a better idea. Will you drive me to Modern Chevrolet Sales in Honaker?"

She answered, "Young lady, you work for Roydon's, not Modern."

"They don't sell cars at Roydon's," I replied.

Artie drove me to Modern that day, and stayed with me until I had signed all the papers. The First National Bank and I were now the proud owners of a used—or, as they say today, preowned—black 1962 Chevrolet Impala. A salesman followed us to Swords Creek and parked the car at Dad's.

Once home, I telephoned Roydon's. I was fortunate. My employer was out of town, and manager, Katie Wells understood my dilemma. She told me to take the day to make other transportation arrangements.

This wasn't easy. There weren't many conveniences in rural southwest Virginia in 1967. We lived in a remote mountainous area where few people owned vehicles. There was a bus line, but I had to be at work by 9 a.m., meaning I had to leave the house by 8:15. My schedule and the bus schedule were hours apart.

I spent the day telephoning. I was no longer going to count on Margaret, no matter her excuse.

In between calls, I sat in "my car." I turned every knob, switched on the ignition, tried the radio, turned the light switch on and off—did everything except drive. I couldn't wait until my sister Frankie came home from school. She had taken driver's education last semester and had her driver's license. I'd probably have to pay her, but she would be my driving instructor.

Dad was employed at VanDyke's Coal Tipple in Swords Creek not far from home. His work shift was over about the same time Frankie arrived from school. She got off the bus at the elementary school and walked home with Dad.

When I saw them walking up the hill, I struck a pose. I slung my arm out the window, leaned back and looked like the cat who ate the canary.

Frankie asked, "Haze, whose car?"

I was bursting with excitement, but I calmly replied, "Mine."

"You don't mean it!" Frankie yelled, running around the shiny Impala.

Dad yelled too, but not in the same tone. "Don't expect me to sign any papers or help pay for that thing!"

90

"Well, just don't expect to park your carcass inside my car!" I yelled back.

My driving lessons proved to be an adventure like none I'd ever experienced, and hopefully never will again. Each afternoon, after work (I'd arranged with my employer to have my hours temporarily coincide with the bus schedule) and school, Frankie and I took the car out for my lessons. Mom stayed home and prayed, but Dad insisted on accompanying us. He usually propped up in the back seat telling us every move to make.

Between Frankie and Dad, how I ever learned to drive a car, I'll never know. Frankie was impatient and bored. Dad made remarks like, "Well, the Virginia Highway Department will save a lot of money this summer. Haze has already scraped the shoulders and cut the brush!"

The day finally arrived when Frankie said I was ready to make my permit. I had studied that little green book from cover to cover, and I had practiced parallel parking until I had it down pat.

We drove to the Richlands National Guard Armory, where both the written and driving tests were conducted. Otis Wilson was the officer who administered the written part. His parents lived near us in Swords Creek, and I'd known Otis my whole life. I felt at ease with him and did extremely well with the written portion. Not so with the driving.

In retrospect, I believe that if Officer Bordon Sawyers had been seated in the back seat, I would have been OK. I was so accustomed to Dad being there. We began by driving around the armory. First thing, I ran over the curb so hard Officer Sawyers bounced on his seat. He advised me to slow the car, and then asked me to give a left hand signal. I put my arm out the window and forgot which was left and right, so I just waved. He was looking out the corner of his eye, and I saw him shaking his head. This was making me more nervous, and the fact that the car's

91

muffler had a hole in it and sounded like a jet airplane didn't help matters.

Frankie was seated with our friend Andy Warner on the back steps of the armory. I came around the corner too fast, skidded and got so close to them that Frankie's dress flipped in the breeze. Andy jumped up, not recognizing me, and asked, "Who is the idiot driving that car?"

"Never saw her before in my life," Frankie answered.

I never did parallel park. I tried. Finally, on my third attempt, Officer Sawyers looked at me and asked, "Honey, you're nervous, aren't you?"

I smiled and answered, "No, of course not!"

"I am," he countered.

I was issued a driver's license solely on the basis of my good written test score.

Driving to work, I sat tall in my Impala and silently thanked Margaret Rickman for the favor she'd done me.

The following winter, I totaled that little black car. I got too close to the shoulder of the road. There was ice and snow on dirt, and when I hit the brakes I flipped the car. The Impala was damaged beyond repair, and I didn't escape injury. My right leg carries a deep scar.

No more dull cars for me. I purchased a maroon 1966 Ford Mustang convertible. I drove home from work the day I purchased it in the spring of 1969. Frankie, a student at Radford College, was home for spring break. We donned silk head scarves and dark glasses, put the top down and went cruisin.'

We drove slowly through Honaker, making sure we were seen. I knew we looked good, but boy we were really getting attention — stares, in fact. I glanced in the rear view mirror, and then I knew why: the trunk lid was up!

Thank God for sunglasses.

I kept that car in mint condition, washed it every other day and waxed it every three months. I married in 1974, and ignoring John's objections, sold the car that following year.

I often wonder where I'd be if I'd kept my Mustang convertible. Bill Clinton kept his!

Teenagers Margaret Rickman and me

Me and my favorite car

What's In a Name?

My dad, Edward Beauchamp Hale, or Beach, as he was addressed, had always hated his name until May, 1971.

This is what happened.

Dad and his friend Frank Vance had driven to Lebanon to the office of Dr. Roy Smith, veterinarian, to purchase "hound medicine," as they called it.

After leaving Dr. Roy's office and heading home, I'm sure they discussed at length the cost of the medicine, how to administer it, and its effectiveness in the treatment of their ailing prized hunting dogs.

As Dad attempted to turn left up the hill toward home, he was probably lighting a Camel cigarette, and Frank was rolling his own with tobacco sprinkled from a Prince Albert tin he kept tucked inside the denim jump jacket he wore winter and summer.

Suddenly, the brightly colored red tin—along with loose tobacco—hit the air when an on-coming car struck Dad's Chevrolet pick-up truck from behind.

Dad, Frank, and the occupant of the car quickly stepped out of the vehicles to inspect damages. Dad's truck had been hit hard and the tailgate was completely crumpled, the taillights shattered, and the rear passenger tire punctured.

The man driving the car was its only occupant, and he introduced himself as Nathan White from West Virginia. Mr. White was visiting family in our area of southwest Virginia, and was frustrated and angry that his sleek maroon colored 1971 Buick Riviera now had a wrecked front grill and bumper, a cracked windshield, and broken headlights. The very vehicle he so proudly had driven to his sister's house only an hour before.

A state trooper was called to the accident scene and Dad swore he had given a signal, and Frank profusely agreed with him. Nathan White strongly contested Dad and Frank's statement resulting in his insurance company refusing to pay for the damages.

So, the case was scheduled for court.

Before the court date, Frank made several visits to our house. Frank was no longer connected to the job force. He received disability Social Security because of damaged lungs caused by underground coal mining. So, he'd come down early and was waiting each evening when Dad arrived home from work. He'd sit patiently while Dad changed his mining clothes, and ate supper.

Then the two of them held long hushed talks on our front porch. Dad gestured and Frank nodded in agreement. Sometimes I'd join them. Between sips of evening coffee, I'd ask, "Dad, are you sure you gave a turn signal before that guy hit you?"

"You're damn right I did! Just ask Frank Vance!"

Frank would cough and take another drag off his cigarette. I'd leave them and go inside to help Mom with dishes. Later, when Frank had gone home and Dad was inside watching television, I'd go back to the porch and sit on the old glider. The faint pleasant smell of Prince Albert tobacco lingered in the air.

The day Dad was to appear in court, Frank came down to the house at 6:00 a.m. Court time was scheduled for 10:00 a.m.!

Frank looked as shiny as a new copper penny. He was clean-shaven, and wore new denim coveralls and a pale blue cotton shirt. I'd seen these on racks at the Company Store, and I knew Dad had driven Frank down there yesterday. I couldn't help but wonder if these items might not appear on Mom's store bill.

Now, this morning Frank, in all his glory, was at our door at 6:00 a.m. Of course, Dad was not working, it being court day. None of us were up. I didn't leave for work until 8:00 a.m., and I was never out of bed before 7:00. Frankie, who arrived home from Radford College a few days earlier, had managed to find a summer job at Jacqueline Manufacturing Company in Richlands. I was employed as bookkeeper for White Front Auto Parts, so she and I rode together.

After Frank roused everyone, Mom started breakfast. When Frankie and I stumbled downstairs, we found a mock court in session.

Dad was questioning Frank. "Mr. Vance, describe in your own words what happened on the afternoon of May 20?"

Frank, looking serious, answered, "Well, sir, it was like this. Me and Mr. Hale was driving up the road minding our own business. Just before we got to our turn-off, Mr. Hale slowed down and gave his signal just like he was supposed to before going up the hill to his house. All of a sudden this big fancy car come a-flyin' out of nowhere and rammed us from behind. Hit us so hard, I lost my Prince Albert tobacco, and that stuff ain't cheap, Your Honor. And my neck still hurts, gives me a fit sometimes."

Mom had stepped into the living room. She handed Dad and Frank coffee, frowned, rolled her eyes at Frankie and me as she passed us seated at the dining room table. We had our hands clapped over our mouths and were shaking all over. We didn't want to laugh out loud, but it was hard to hold. The scene being played out in the living room was better than any television program.

Dad, between sips of coffee, advised Frank, "Well, pretty good, but I wouldn't mention tobacco or back pain. The judge might not smoke, and he could think I want a bunch of money if you talk about pain. I just want to be cleared of this thing. At my age, I don't want anything going against my record. I sure don't want my license suspended or my insurance raised, especially since I'm leaving work next year."

Frankie and I headed upstairs because we couldn't hold the laughter much longer. We dressed for work, grabbed a cup of Mom's delicious just-perked coffee on our way out, hugged them — and Frank — and made for my car.

At the foot of the hill, I turned right instead of left.

"Where are we going?" yelled Frankie. "Richlands is in the other direction!" Then she smiled as it dawned on her.

"We're going to the court house in Lebanon," I nodded. "I wouldn't miss this for a week's wages."

We waited until the last minute to slip in unnoticed and sat in back.

"All arise please. Judge Beauchamp presiding."

I could have sworn I saw Frank's new denim coveralls shake as he stood. Dad stood ramrod straight. He was called first to testify.

The opening question put to him by the judge: "Did you or did you not have your turn signal operating at the time of the accident?"

"I sure did, Your Honor. And I believe I put my arm out the window and gave a manual signal as well. Years ago when I made my permit, that's how it was done, you know."

The judge was taking notes, but then he dropped his fountain pen and looked at Dad. "Mr. Hale, was your father Robert Franklin Hale?"

"Yes sir, I'm proud to say he was."

Judge Beauchamp pulled off his glasses and leaned back in his chair. "Well now, this is interesting. I believe your father named you in honor of my father, Judge Alonzo Beauchamp. The two of them were best friends."

Mr. White dropped in his seat like begonias after a heavy frost.

Following a lengthy testimony from Dad, Frank, and Mr. White, the gavel sounded, and Judge Beauchamp declared, "I rule in favor of the defendant. All charges dismissed."

Frankie and I quickly left the courtroom before Dad or Frank saw us. We drove to our jobs, worked a half-shift, and once home that afternoon innocently listened as Dad and Frank gloated about the trial.

Dad began, "Girls, have I ever told you how I got my name? I've changed my mind about not liking it. It was always so hard to spell when I started school, and the kids made fun of it."

I played along. "Didn't Grandpa Hale name you in honor of a good friend?"

Dad swaggered across the porch. "Sure did. And his name was Judge Alonzo Beauchamp. You know, my dad knew some pretty important people."

Mom was seated on the swing, and she looked as if she could kick Dad every time she swung close to him.

Frank was seated on the top porch step struggling to roll a cigarette. He finally succeeded and rolled the cigarette, twisted the edges, and licked it in order to seal the thin white paper.

Dad joined Frank on the steps and continued his account of the trial. "Well, I answered as honest as I knew how."

Mom snorted, "You're the one, all right. The very one God will welcome with open arms. He'll say, 'Enter in my good and faithful servant. Your honesty has won you a crown of righteousness.'"

Dad turned his head in her direction so fast that I'm sure if he hadn't already suffered a whiplash from the accident, he had one now. "Just keep your jib out of this! I'm tryin' to tell the girls what happened in court today."

"As *honestly* as you know how," Mom mocked.

If looks could kill, my mother would have dropped out of that swing like a fly on the end of a swatter.

"Girls," Dad continued, "the judge there today was Alonzo Beauchamp's son, and he remembered how his dad and mine were best friends. Not that it had any bearing on the trial, mind you, but I guess he felt pretty good knowing my dad had named me in honor of his dad."

Mom had crossed her legs and was pushing the swing with one foot. When upset, she had a habit of shaking her foot, and she was giving her free one a gymnastic work out, keeping time with the rhythm of the swing as it swung back and forth.

"Well, how did he rule, Dad?" Frankie asked, leaning forward in mock anticipation of his answer.

Dad pulled his cigarettes from his shirt pocket, enjoying delaying the suspense. Soon Camel smoke mingled with Prince Albert smoke as he triumphantly answered, "That man ruled in my favor! And I'm damned proud to be called Beauchamp."

We sat around for another twenty minutes or so, allowing Dad and Frank time to bask in the warm glow of victory.

Later, when Frank said his goodbyes and headed up the hill toward home, Mom threatened Dad, "You'd better fork over the money you charged to my Company Store account for Frank's new clothes, or your might not be so lucky at your next court appearance, *Beauchamp* Hale!"

Dad at his home—1971

Frank Vance at his home—1971

An Uncommon Woman

In her younger day, Louise Combs May Wilson Shoman was a beauty. With coal black hair, olive skin and a brilliant smile, she may have been Ava Gardner's sister. But she wasn't; she was my mother's younger sister.

The youngest of six children, Louise was born in 1922 in Honaker, Virginia, to Will and Ada (Craft) Combs. My grandfather, who was twenty years older than Granny, became ill and unable to work when Louise was three years old. Granny worked in a sewing room doing alterations to support the family. Her meager salary covered bare necessities, so Louise never knew what it was to own new clothes. However, on her, even hand-me-downs looked good.

Outgoing, athletic and competitive, she was something to see as she skated, played basketball or danced. She excelled in everything requiring coordination and balance, including climbing through her bedroom window to attend dances. My grandparents were strict, but that didn't stop her. Her motto: "Where there's a will, there's a way," or in her case, "Where there's a window, there's escape."

It was at one of those forbidden dances that she met the love of her life — tall, handsome, much older and divorced Ruey May. He literally swept her off her feet, and at age 17, she married him and moved to Howard, Ohio, to begin her new life on a dairy/vegetable farm. Ruey hired on as manager, and Louise worked by his side from daylight until dark. She canned, preserved, cleaned and cooked—all the things, and then some, to help keep the huge farm operating smoothly.

During the first years of their marriage, two sons were born. The boys were handsome. With parents such as theirs, Jim and John had no other choice.

Hard work and happiness walked hand in hand until Louise discovered Ruey had a roving eye. Completely crushed, she packed her bags and left. The boys, ages 18 and 16, were old enough to be without her. With no place to go, she lived with her brother, Earlie, and his family in Newark, Ohio, for several months. She placed ads in local newspapers that read, "Will live in and care for invalids." An elderly couple responded, and she lived with them until their deaths three years later.

She now had enough money saved to rent an apartment. Excited about having her own place, she eagerly set about furnishing and decorating it. During this time, she called my mother and anxiously told her, "Effie, I'm overdoing it. I'm feeling dizzy, my vision is poor and I'm forever dropping things."

Mom, always a worrier, said, "Louise, see a doctor, and don't put it off!"

Some time later, a devastated Louise called to say she had been diagnosed with multiple sclerosis. She was 39 years old.

Still active, she continued to bowl and worked several jobs, one of which was as a cook in a restaurant in Mt. Vernon. She met her second husband, C.B. Wilson, in the restaurant. After a whirlwind courtship, she married him.

I believe she was tired of fending for herself and realized the outlook for the future wasn't the best. C. B. vowed that her illness didn't diminish his love for her.

During her married life with this man, we saw little of her, and heard less. She was married to him for three years when she telephoned us, "C.B. was run over by a train. He isn't expected to live." There wasn't an ounce of grief in her voice. His home was mortgaged to the hilt; even his car was sold as payment toward the outrageous debts he'd been accumulating all his life.

On her own again, with nothing except a devastating illness, she applied for and received federal aid. She moved into a low-rent apartment complex and lived comfortably. An inspiration to multiple sclerosis sufferers, she attended support meetings. Soon she was elected chairman of the Columbus, Ohio Multiple Sclerosis Society.

Now she could walk only with the assistance of a walker and leg braces. Her sons purchased a specially designed car for her so she was able to drive.

I spent the summer of 1974 with her, and she amazed me. She never felt sorry for herself, and continued to be active. If she couldn't waltz or bowl or skate, she could play poker. And win! Poker parties were regular at her apartment on Friday nights. Always, she baked. She never forgot the farm days, and she baked her famous cherry pies or chocolate cakes. She was the most popular tenant in the building, with everyone crowding into her apartment on Friday nights for poker and dessert.

During her quiet moments, she was reflective. Once she asked me, "Will you play my favorite record?" I obliged, and soon Ernest Tubb's "Waltz Across Texas" floated through the apartment.

"If he had just lived," she repeated for the third time — "he" being Ruey. The year before, after his wife had died, he and Louise had begun seeing each other. "I never stopped loving him," she confessed. "I worked my fingers to the bone for him, but I couldn't take his unfaithfulness." She seemed to look right past me, and then shook her head as she continued, "But, you know, he had changed. The years had mellowed him."

Motioning for me to help her remove her leg brace, she sighed and closed her eyes. "That was our song. Why did he have to die so suddenly? He never told me he had a heart condition. He never said anything."

I was sorry to leave her at summer's end. She was so full of life, yet I worried about the disease handicapping her more.

But she didn't give up. Two years later, Louise married a third time, this time to a wonderful man, Russell Shoman. Russ was a widower, a father of seven children with grandchildren everywhere. He and his family were good to her. A daughter, Sandy, drove them lots of places. As long as Louise was able to travel, they made several trips from Ohio to Virginia visiting her hometown, and she and Mom had wonderful visits. Also, they traveled to Canada, Mexico, or any place she cared to see until the multiple sclerosis completely controlled her. Louise and Russ had several years together until he died in 1995. Louise followed in 1996.

My father was seriously ill at the time Louise died, and it grieved me that I couldn't travel to Ohio for her funeral. My cousin, Louise's son, John, called me after he returned to his home in South Carolina. He related to me an absolutely fascinating story. He began by asking, "Hazel, did you visit my Dad's grave when you were in Ohio in '74?"

"Yes," I answered, recalling that visit I made with Aunt Louise shortly before I left. "I thought it a beautiful place. I loved the pond and the trees. Why do you ask?"

I could hear John breathe deeply as he continued. "Some time ago, Russ had a winning raffle ticket. The prize was a cemetery plot. We used this plot to bury Mom, since Russ was buried beside his first wife. Do you have any idea where this plot is located?"

Of course I had no clue.

John's voice, trembling with emotion, hung on the wire as he continued, "It's located right beside my Dad. Mom is buried in Mt. Vernon Cemetery **beside Dad**!"

I was stunned.

After a moment's silence, I softly replied, "Aunt Louise always said, 'Where there's a will, there's a way.' Perhaps they're waltzing around heaven."

Louise Combs — Honaker, VA

Of Families, Friends, and Fiascos

Harvesting Memories

I was filled with impatience on this particular July day back in 1984, and couldn't wait to exchange my air-conditioned neon-lighted office for fresh air and sunshine.

When six o'clock finally arrived, I headed to the parking lot with co-workers. During our walk, I took orders for tomatoes and green beans from mine and Dad's vegetable garden. Lib Jessee joked if this continued I'd need a license and corner stand!

My husband was employed as a heavy equipment operator for Island Creek Coal Company, and during summer months it wasn't unusual for him to work until 9:00, sometimes 10:00 p.m. I complained, even when John explained that his type work must be completed during nice weather.

Our son was married and gone, and even though I had my own job, I needed something to fill my time during the long summer evenings. That's why I began gardening with Dad. He was an excellent gardener, and I think it pleased him that I wanted to help tend the soil. But there were times I wished I'd never begun this endeavor.

Dad was a hard taskmaster. He had certain ways to do things, and it was his way or no way. For instance, Dad insisted that rows for planting be perfectly straight. To achieve this, he'd tie fodder twine around a stake driven at one end of the garden, and pull it across to another stake. He'd then "lay off" rows by following the twine. He used that old lay-off plow the way a painter used a brush to create a masterpiece.

Dad didn't allow border flowerbeds. "Just a waste of good ground," he'd scoff as Mom and I argued with him. This summer I outdid him and planted morning glory seed between rows of corn.

"They are right pretty," he reluctantly admitted as he sat on his front porch steps early one morning and viewed purple and pink winding their way up green corn stalks.

Dad had a sixth sense about when to plant. Unlike his wife and neighbors, he didn't plant according to "signs" Mom read in *The Old Farmer's Almanac*. She wouldn't trim a rose bush without first consulting her faithful guide, and was appalled that Dad didn't do the same with his gardening.

This spring when he and I had the seed potatoes ready, Mom called to us from the porch. "You'd better not plant those now! The signs are in the bowels!"

Dad leaned in on his hoe handle and called back, "I don't care if they &#%# all over the patch! I'm plantin' my potatoes!"

By early July we'd already dug "new potatoes" and from all indications, we'd have a pretty good crop this fall.

This evening as I turned up the hill leading to Mom and Dad's, I was pleased to see my sister Frankie's car in the driveway. I parked, and as I exited, I heard a commotion coming from the cucumber patch. I looked to see Frankie's young children, nine-year-old Spencer, and seven-year-old Jessica, running through the patch toward the house.

Dad was after them.

"You young'uns! You've trampled my cucumber and melon vines. I'd better not catch you in here again."

Frankie, interrupted from helping Mom prepare supper, stepped through the door. She saw me, waved, and motioned me to sit beside her in the old metal glider. "Some things never change," she remarked.

I removed dark glasses, placed a hand on the glider's cool armrest, and chuckled as I watched Dad and her children. "Spencer and Jessica are more fortunate though. Dad has slowed down from the times he chased us from his garden. Sometimes we didn't get away."

Frankie nodded in agreement. "Yeah, and that meant no Saturday night television."

I removed my high heels, stretched my suntanned legs, and giggled. "But Dad didn't know we had just as much fun upstairs playing Old Maid."

We were distracted from reminiscing as Spencer and Jessica, now on the porch, raced for the wooden slat swing. Dad followed, and wiped his face with the back of his hand before sitting opposite us.

They swung the swing high, and then Spencer dragged his feet across the porch to slow it. He solemnly declared to his grandfather, "I don't like you, I never have liked you, and never will like you."

Dad was taken aback, but quickly regained his composure. "Well, little man, I don't care. You're still not going to play hide and seek in my garden!"

Jessica slid from the swing, walked across the porch, and put both arms around Dad's neck. She nuzzled her face against his and told him, "I love you, Grandpa."

Dad cleared his throat, hugged Jessica, and in a husky voice told us he was going inside to wash up for supper.

Once he'd closed the door behind him, Frankie winked at me. We both understood how much Jessica's gesture had meant to Dad. And how he'd always remember what Spencer had said. Poor Spencer!

Through the screen door, we heard Mom raise her voice. We knew she was giving Dad a hard time because he'd scolded the children. She soon came out, fanning herself with an apron. Dad refused to have air-conditioning installed, and the heat from the kitchen had left Mom flushed.

"Sometimes I wish he'd just throw up a tent and live in that darn garden. And young lady," she said to me, "you didn't help matters when you began helping him. Your dad's gotten fanatical about it."

Mom had a habit of rocking fast when she was aggravated, and she was giving that old rocker a real workout. "Oh, that breeze feels good!" she said. "I'm glad the beans aren't finished cooking. I need a rest."

Frankie told Mom we all felt the breeze from her rocker, and we continued joking around. Then Mom called to Dad, "Beach, while you're in the kitchen, check the beans!"

After a minute, we heard a noise like thunder followed by Dad bursting through the door. He ran up and down the steps shaking his fist at Mom, accusing her of trying to kill him. His face was fiery red, and blisters were forming.

Spencer and Jessica jumped off the porch, and were once again in the garden. Only this time, they were hiding! Frankie, Mom, and I grabbed Dad and forced him to sit.

"What's wrong with you? And what's happened to your face?" Mom asked over and over.

Dad glared at her, moaned, and covered his face.

Frankie and I hurried to the kitchen and saw an unbelievable sight. The kitchen was a wreck. Mom had been cooking green beans in a pressure cooker, and when she'd asked Dad to check them, he'd jerked off the lid! Green beans were everywhere, all over the stove, the walls, and the floor. Above the stove there was a gaping hole in the ceiling. The pressure must have blown the lid completely out of his hands and sent it through the plaster.

We rushed back to Mom and Dad. I quickly examined his hands and arms, relieved and surprised he still had them. Frankie found ointment for burns and went to work on Dad's face.

"Please, Daddy, you need to get to the hospital. Mom can keep the children, and we'll take you," Frankie pleaded.

"I ain't goin' to no hospital!"

"My goodness, Beach, when I asked you to check the beans, I thought you knew I meant for you to tell me if the cooker was jingling."

Dad jumped up again, and yelled, "Jingle, hell!"

Frankie dropped the tube of ointment, looked at me, and we both ran down the steps and joined Spencer and Jessica in the garden. We laughed until we rolled in Dad's cucumber patch.

For several days Dad's face was blistered and pock-marked. The burning beans had hit his face so hard they'd left imprints in the shape of beans. He escaped scarring because Mom carefully bandaged his wounds and saw to it that he stayed out of the garden and hot sun until he was completely healed.

Dad and I continued to "raise gardens" until he was eighty-three. That spring he suffered a major stroke. He recovered, but not enough to work in his beloved garden. John and I struggled to maintain one that summer, but without Dad's uncanny know-how, it was a complete failure.

Today John is retired, my parents gone, and I spend more time at my computer than in a garden. But it takes only the jingle of my pressure cooker to take me home . . .

. . . back to our warm, sunny garden, working alongside my dad.

Dad and one of his gardens

Partners in crime — Spencer and Jessica

EBY

My dad often remarked that he had 100 sons-in-law, a one and two zeros. Unfortunately, my husband, John, wasn't the glorified ONE. Dad's attitude angered me, and I would allow this anger to simmer until it reached the boiling point. Then, I'd tell Dad in no uncertain terms that I felt he was completely wrong to make such statements even if they were, as he claimed, in fun. John ignored them, and continued being at Dad's beck and call.

I kept telling John, "I just dare you to run down there every time Dad wants something. Let him call number one!"

My good-natured husband, even after working a grueling 12-hour shift at Island Creek Coal Company, sometimes helped Dad in the garden until after dark. Yet, at every family gathering, Dad praised number one to the skies. John and then fellow zero brother-in-law, Terry, only winked at each other while my sister, Frankie, and I wanted to throw something at Dad.

We made parting remarks, "Don't call us, we're not worthy." Or, "You'd better mention your blind spot to Dr. Scott. It's getting worse."

Poor Mom didn't know what to think of all this, and neither did J. B., son-in-law number one. J. B.'s wife, my sister Nadine, could care less. Besides, Dad *helped* them!

The straw that almost broke the camel's back occurred September, 1985. Here's what happened.

Garnett Ray, an outspoken family friend, once told Dad, "Beach, you might not go to hell for a dollar, but you'll mess around the edge and fall in." It was well known that Dad loved money, and he never failed to preach his philosophy: "I get just as much pleasure from saving a dollar as most people do spending one."

For example, in 1972, realizing that he would soon be declared totally disabled to work, he bought a new Chevrolet step side pick up truck. He only made the first two payments, and then his insurance kicked in and paid the balance. He *loved* this, but just couldn't understand why HE should be responsible for the truck's maintenance. He shrewdly escaped that too.

Well aware that one of his zero sons-in-law loved vehicles, and was a terrific mechanic, he whined to John, who, in turn kept the truck's oil changed and motor tuned. In exchange, Dad bragged about how much money J. B. had earned the previous year. This stood my auburn hair on end, and when John mentioned to me that Dad's truck tires needed changing, I yelled, "Don't even think about it!"

A worried John answered, "But those tires are slick as ribbons and I'm afraid he's going to wreck and kill himself and your mom. He can't half drive anyway."

This caught my attention, and that evening after work, I drove down home. On my way, I calculated how to approach Dad. I knew if I said, "Dad, you need new truck tires," he'd mentally see dollars floating away, and tell me to mind my own business. I had to convince him he could save money by purchasing new tires.

As I pulled into the driveway, Dad was seated on his comfortable porch swing. I normally bounced up the steps, but today I slowly walked around his truck.

"What's the matter?" Dad called, leaving the swing to join me.

"Oh, just looking at your tires," I mused and continued my inspection.

"What's wrong with them? They're damn good tires, gets me and Effie there and back."

Ignoring him, I removed a dime from my purse, and placed it between a tire's worn tread. The entire dime was visible.

"Dad, come here!"

Pulling a Camel cigarette from his shirt pocket, he took his time lighting it. He knelt beside me, and I think, deliberately blew smoke in my face.

"What'd you want?"

"See this dime?"

"Yeah. What about it?"

"I'll tell you what about it. There's not enough tread on these raggedy-ass tires to get you off the hill, much less anyplace else. Dad, you're going to get fined—big time!"

"Ah, you don't know what you're talking about," Dad grumbled, but he had removed his cap and was scratching his head, a sure sign he was worried.

"I reckon I do. A girl who works with me was fined $500 for driving on tires a lot better looking than these dilapidated 13-year-old babies."

I followed him to the porch, and Mom joined us. It didn't take much to convince her that I was right, and she vowed then and there she wouldn't step foot back in that truck until four new tires were put on.

"Now see what you've done!" Dad accused me as I hugged him goodbye and departed for home.

Once home, I telephoned J. B., and explained the truck tire situation. He agreed to support me when Dad called questioning about the penalty for driving on worn tires. I'd hoped J. B. would offer help.

The following morning, Saturday, John and I usually slept in. Not this time. We were jolted from our bed by the early insistent ringing of the phone.

"You answer it," I told him and rolled over to hide a smile. The action had begun.

"Yeah, Beach, I'll drive you to Bristol, but you'll be just as well off to let Bill Chambers put four new tires on your truck. I read that ad too, but I believe the sale was for thirteen-inch, not fifteen-inch, the size you need. Well, all right. I'll be down as soon as I eat breakfast."

During breakfast, John told me Dad had phoned J. B. who told him the Bristol Kmart had a half-price today-only tire sale. "I tried to tell him," John said, "the sale is for thirteen-inch, but he won't listen."

Five hours later, John stormed into the kitchen, yelling, "This is it! I will *never* do another thing for that man! Never! Mark my word!"

"I hate to say, 'I told you so,' but I told you so.'"

"Not another word. I'll tell you later."

After washing his car, John came to the patio door, and asked me to join him. He noticed my hesitation. "Oh, I've worked out the frustration."

Sipping a cold drink, he began to talk about it. "You won't believe what a day I've had. Your dad sulked all the way to Bristol. I tried to make conversation, but he'd only say things like, "Wish to heck I'd never seen that truck. I'll tell you what a man needs—a good saddle horse." I'll bet he smoked a whole pack of cigarettes. With all my allergies, I feel like I've been shell-shocked."

"Let me tell you, after we got to Kmart, things became worse. I was right. The sale was for thirteen-inch tires. Beach walked around that big store at least five times before finally agreeing to buy fifteen-inch tires."

"When the clerk wrote his receipt, he asked, 'What's your name, sir?'"

"'E. B. Hale,' your dad yelled. He'd said it so fast, and in such a hateful voice, the clerk couldn't understand him, so he politely asked, 'I beg your pardon, sir?'"

"This time Beach repeated it three times, and each time faster, 'E. B. Hale, E. B. Hale, E. B. Hale,' and I thought he was never going to count out the money — fumbled around in that fat wallet — like to have embarrassed me to death."

"When Beach finally paid the clerk, and had the receipt in his hand, I got him out of the store and into the service department. While the tires were being put on and balanced, your dad grabbed his chest and began wheezing. 'John, I'm going to have to take one of my nitroglycerin pills.'"

"I ran down the street and got him a drink from a vending machine. I had him sit and take the pill. He wiped his face with that big red bandana handkerchief he always carries, and groaned, 'Damn, that's a whole lot of money.'"

"After he calmed down a little, I asked to see the receipt. I knew it! The clerk had written EBY Hale instead of E. B. I turned my head. I sure didn't want "Eby" to see me laugh, not at a time like this. I'll tell you, Haze, by the time I got him home, *I* needed a heart pill!"

"This is it! No more! No More!"

After this declaration, the radiator hose went bad on Dad's truck, then the manifold pipe, muffler, and tailpipe.

Guess who came to the rescue?

Dad with sons-in-law John and J.B., And former son-in-law, Terry

John and me — mid 1970s

The Last Chase

"Girls, run that old dog off the porch!" Mom had just scrubbed the front porch, and as usual, Lou felt it was her signal to snuggle behind the metal glider for her afternoon nap.

"Frankie, you do it!"

"I will not! I remember the last time I chased Lou off the porch." Thirteen-year-old Frankie stuck out her lower lip — a sure sign she wouldn't change her mind.

And I did understand.

Dad's uproar could be heard bouncing off the mountains. Our close neighbors came running, thinking one of us had suffered an accident.

I honestly believe Dad and his hound dogs, especially Lou, had a secret way of communicating. Dad could be miles away from home working for Pocahontas Fuel Company in Amonate, but when he arrived home, he'd know if one of his hounds had been touched.

During the sixties, my teenage years, Dad's prized black and tan Walker hounds had the run of the place, and we hated it. Mom, Granny Combs, Frankie, and I were kept busy chasing them off porches, and out of flower beds. A few of them even tried to enter the house each time a door was opened.

Dad complained, but we kept on chasing them.

The peculiar thing, I can never remember them doing damage to Dad's garden. It seemed they knew how hard Dad worked to grow vegetables. They respected him and stayed away.

123

At one time I counted fourteen adult hounds and a whole slew of puppies. We may have hated dealing with the adults, but there's nothing more adorable than a hound puppy. As children, Frankie and I played with them for hours. We dressed them in doll clothes, put them in our wagon and pulled them all over the neighborhood. People cooed as they looked at those little wrinkled faces wrapped in frilly bonnets.

There were two adult hounds who stood still while we played "beauty shop." Fly and Sadie. They seemed to enjoy having their toe-nails painted bright red. They didn't mind at all when we roped imitation pearls around their necks and clipped large earrings to their ears.

Afterward, Mom soaked her jewelry in order to remove the dog smell. She said she wouldn't be surprised if, while sitting in church, a big tick crawled up her neck off the strand of pearls. She'd warn us never to do it again. We'd take our scolding and nod; two days later Fly and Sadie would prance around dressed to kill.

Dad had a reputation among the foxhunting set. People said he owned "Some of the best dogs in the country." And, "When it comes to dogs, that man knows how to raise 'em!"

This reputation wasn't just local. It gained momentum, and hunters from Tennessee and Kentucky were soon knocking on our door. I was fourteen when Dad traded a hound and fifty dollars for Mom's first electric stove. From that moment, each time Mom fussed about his hounds, Dad had this to say, "Just shut up about my dogs. You wouldn't have that big fancy stove if it wasn't for them."

Mom knew it, but she still grumbled.

I was sixteen when one of Dad's barber customers kicked Lou.

Dad and his buddies usually had their big chase Friday night, and the poor dogs came home Saturday morning as worn out as their masters.

This July Saturday morning Frankie, Mom, and I were trying to clean house. Dad was busy reliving a fox chase and talking up the then popular "crew cut." Suddenly, we heard Dad's angry voice. Lou, now aged, but still bravely chasing fox, had run hard the night before and was curled up in her favorite spot behind the glider. Stuart Hale, seated on the glider, awaiting his turn in the barber chair, kicked Lou when she rubbed against his leg.

Dad laid down his hair clippers, walked over to Stuart, and in an icy, deadly voice said, "I've got a wife and two daughters in the house, if you want to kick something. You so much as touch that dog again, and I'll blow your damn brains out."

Dad wouldn't have allowed anyone to harm us, but we knew what he meant.

Dad was heartbroken when his mother died in 1953, but I don't think he grieved any less in 1964, the day Artie Rickman telephoned from her store asking him to "Walk down the hill."

I went with him. There by the side of the road lay his beloved Lou.

She had been coming home from a fox chase, crossed the highway and been struck and killed by a vehicle driven by a friend's son, Larry Ball. Larry hadn't left the scene, and he kept apologizing and telling Dad he tried to miss her, but she was directly in front of his car.

Dad didn't say a word. He bent and gently picked up Lou and carried her home, tears streaming down his face. Once home, he wrapped her in our best blanket and buried her at the edge of our garden. He placed stones at the head of her grave and Frankie and I wrote her name on one of the stones.

Dad continued to "raise hounds" and fox hunt for many years following Lou's death. However, old age forced him to sell his dogs in 1989, the year he turned eighty. He said to me, "I'm not able to climb these hills, and I ain't about to punish my dogs. They need to be turned loose."

September, 1992, at age eighty-three, Dad suffered a severe stroke.

After he recovered enough to be released from the hospital, Frankie thought if he had a hound pup to love, it would help speed his full recovery. With this thought, she purchased a pup from O. B. Lockhart, who, as a young man had accompanied Dad on several hunts.

Dad's eyes became two bright stars when he first saw this beautiful pup, but he soon lost interest. I knew then he would never recover his full mental and physical capabilities. Sadly, we returned the pup to O. B., who grieved along with us.

Later that same year, Mom passed away. My sisters and I refused to even entertain the idea of having Dad put in a nursing facility. We hired in-home help to stay through the week, and Nadine, Frankie, and I took turns staying each weekend. We never left him alone, even for a few minutes.

Still, one night while Frankie was staying with him, he managed to unlock the front door and slip out unnoticed. Frankie was sleeping upstairs, and thought she had the door securely locked, so Dad, who slept in a hospital bed downstairs, would be okay. As she later told me, the insistent ringing of the 'phone awakened her from a deep sleep. Stumbling, almost falling down the stairs, she answered.

"Who's calling at three a.m.?" Frankie demanded.

"Ma'am, this is the Russell County Sheriff's Department, and we believe we have your father here in the squad car with us."

"No, you don't have my daddy. He's sleeping in the next room."

"Check his bed, ma'am."

Wide awake now, a panicked Frankie yelled, "It's pouring rain! Where in the world did you find him?"

Dad had gotten out of bed, dressed, managed to unlock the door, and walked two miles through Call Valley to his favorite hunting spot. Finally, he became so exhausted, he sat in the middle of the road. A man driving a large truck almost hit him. This man put him in his truck and located authorities, who questioned Dad.

My dad, who by then couldn't tell you his age, and who still thought Mom was coming home from the hospital, correctly told the police officer his telephone number, his daughter's names and addresses, how long he'd lived in his neighborhood, and even directed him to his house.

After he was changed into dry clothes and once again put to bed, Frankie asked, "Daddy, why did you do this?"

Dad grinned and said, "It's been a long time since me and ol' Lou went huntin.'"

The following morning as Frankie was helping Dad from his bed, he moaned and exclaimed, "I don't why in this world my old legs hurt so bad."

Frankie answered, "Daddy, do you think it has anything to do with you walking all over Swords Creek and back last night?"

He'd already forgotten.

Frankie presenting Dad with a hound pup

One of Dad's hounds on the front porch

A Daffodil Day

Saturday, March 8 was an incredibly beautiful day. I breathed in crisp air, and felt warmed by the sun as it dominated a sky the color of my granddaughter Kayla's eyes.

To take advantage of the wonderful weather, and my feeling of well-being, I telephoned Kayla. "Hey, sky-blue, how about spending the day with me?"

"MaMaw, where did you get a name like that for Kayla?"

I laughed and told her to never mind, but I'd see her soon.

At age eleven, Kayla was most happy "doing something." She became easily bored, so I had several things planned. As I drove into her driveway, I felt I had the day scheduled the way she liked.

Leaving Cedar Bluff at ten, we drove to North Tazewell and visited my aunt Belle. Kayla loved thumbing through Aunt Belle's scrapbooks, and Aunt Belle enjoyed weaving stories around old photos. I'd heard them hundreds of times, but I always came away with a filled notepad, and a tinfoil-wrapped German chocolate cake.

Following our visit, I stopped by Outback Hair Studio and my hairdresser, Gloria, gave Kayla the works—shampoo, conditioner, cut, and style.

It was now lunch time, and on to Kayla's "favorite place in the whole wide world," Kentucky Fried Chicken. I hated to admit it, but after lunch, I just wanted to go home, curl up, and sleep.

But Kayla was full of energy, eager to show off her new hairdo, so I searched my mind for something else to do. For no reason, my friend Kathleen's words flashed before me. "Mrs. Busic is getting so frail."

Mrs. Busic, a retired high school English and Latin teacher who lived alone, was our community's favorite storyteller. Until recently, she substituted teaching, shared her wonderful stories and poems at practically every area event, and was a regular contributor for a local newspaper. This changed as her health declined.

I stopped by a supermarket and purchased a dozen fresh-baked doughnuts and a quart of strawberries. Kayla, thinking these were hers, reached in the bag. "Oh MaMaw, you're the best!"

"Stay out of them! They're not for you!" I snapped. The strain of pre-teen company was beginning to manifest itself.

The hurt look on her face spoke more than words. I quickly explained that we were taking them to Mrs. Busic. I talked about her, and by the time we arrived at the old colonial two-story, Kayla was anxious to meet her.

Daffodils lined the way to the back door. Today must be the day for insight, I mused. Just as I was about to knock, I thought of Mrs. Busic's poem, "My Friend's Daughter." Her friend's daughter shied away from hugging her, and although she, Mrs. Busic, pretended indifference, the hurt was intense.

I smiled at Kayla. She wasn't shy, but she might not think of it herself. "When we say good-bye to Mrs. Busic, give her a big hug, and tell her you love her."

As Kayla nodded, the clothes she was wearing all day came into focus. "Honey, did you *have* to wear those shiny black hip boots and miniskirt?"

Kayla just flipped her glossy hair and grinned as I knocked on the door. I knocked several times, and received no reply. However, I saw a note taped to the door directing the local pharmacist to leave a prescription on the kitchen table. I knew then that the door was unlocked, so we entered the house.

We found Mrs. Busic seated in her old recliner, a blanket up to her chin, snoozing. I gently shook her, and she looked at us and smiled.

"Brought you something," I said.

She was delighted to see us, and even more delighted that I remembered her love for doughnuts.

"I'll have one now. I can't remember if I've eaten today."

She ate as if indeed she hadn't eaten a bite of food the entire day.

I introduced Kayla to her, adding, "She enjoys dressing in wild clothes."

As Mrs. Busic reached for Kayla's hand, she gave me a "teacher" look and said in a stern voice, "She has the courage to be different. I like this."

She patted Kayla's hand, smiled, and told her, "Kayla, I love your boots. I've always had a desire to wear short skirts and boots, but with a chicken body like mine, I never could."

A beaming Kayla was won over.

I meekly sat beside Mrs. Busic and asked her to please tell stories. "Just make sure you keep that pad and pen inside your handbag," she warned as she playfully shook her finger.

She settled more comfortably in her chair and began. A usually super-active Kayla sat transfixed listening to Mrs. Busic's magical tales. I knew what was coming, but Kayla had no idea. When Mrs. Busic did her famous witch cackle, Kayla almost leaped from her seat.

I excused myself while Mrs. Busic and Kayla became better acquainted, and busied myself in the kitchen. I washed dishes, swept, and wiped down the table and countertops. I then prepared the strawberries the way Mrs. Busic liked, sprinkled with sugar. How fresh they looked in the sparkle of her cut glass bowl. She shared with Kayla, and the three of us visited another hour.

When it was time to leave, Kayla crossed the room, and hugged Mrs. Busic. "Thank you for telling me those wonderful stories. I'll never forget them, and I won't forget you." She leaned over and kissed her new friend.

Tears formed in Mrs. Busic's eyes, and she said to Kayla, "Always be true to yourself, and you will be happy."

She asked us to help her stand, and once on her feet, she walked with us to the door. I commented on her beautiful daffodils.

She thanked me and said she'd love some to place on her clean table. "Kayla, do you mind? Uneven numbers, please. Don't ever use even numbers for flower arrangements! Remember that."

As Kayla picked flowers, something made me ask Mrs. Busic if she liked turnips and cornbread. "Yes, I love them. Are you going to bring them?"

I promised I would.

"Well, if you do, put sugar in the turnips as you cook them."

Why, of all the nerve, I thought. Here I am, willing to cook the things, and she tells me how! I smiled knowing she'd never change.

She looked so frail standing in the doorway. "Don't you think it's time you had someone with you? I worry that you may fall while getting in and out of bed."

"Well, I hate to forego my independence."

"Oh, you'd never do that! You can teach someone else about sugar in the turnips."

We were interrupted as Kayla proudly handed Mrs. Busic nine perfectly cut daffodils. We repeated good-byes and Kayla and I walked down the back steps to the car.

Impulsively, I asked Kayla to remain in the car while I went back for a minute.

I found her standing by the door where we'd left her. I hugged her, and determined to make her laugh, said, "You stubborn old thing! I love you anyway."

She lightly touched my face. "You could have been my daughter-in-law."

Rolling my eyes in mock distress, I exclaimed, "Have mercy!"

This time, the twinkle reappeared in her faded eyes, and I heard a genuine Georgia Busic chuckle.

"Get your beautiful granddaughter home, but come again. Soon."

She stood there bathed in sunlight clutching her daffodils.

I like to think that's how Heaven welcomed her, April 4, 1997.

My Friend's Daughter
by
Georgia I. Busic

She was beautiful standing in the doorway,
For she had her dad's dancing eyes and ready smile
(I had loved her Mom and Dad for quite awhile)
There was something whimsical and sweet about her –
Just like her Mom!
I moved instinctively, impulsively to embrace her;
For a hug is sometimes the only word I know to say,
And it is usually the only word I need to say
But she somehow recoiled and moved to stand beside her mom.

Now I knew why she didn't want me to touch her;
She saw only wrinkles, the age signs, the years.
She didn't understand the love I feel—the loneliness, the fears,
And how I long each day for something alive to touch;
Yet, she was a sweet young thing—polite, talkative –
The very kind of daughter I'd want to have
Were I so fortunate as to have a daughter of my own.

I somehow felt she was right,
I learned a lesson that night;

133

For I suddenly remembered
How my mom used to make me
Give Aunt Wanda a kiss and a big hug to Uncle Kyle
While I shied away from their thin white hair and toothless
smile.

Well, I haven't been the same since that night.
I guess I'll never be the same again.
From now on I'll offer a handshake,
warm, sincere, polite
But I'll wait for the other person
To initiate a hug, if a hug be right.

Note: Mrs. Busic's son, Eldridge granted permission to print above poem.

Georgia Busic—honored guest at a class reunion

Kayla shown with her paternal grandfather, John, and sister Katie
—1997

One Wild Ride

Autumn 1995 was exceptionally dry and hot. The weekend of September 22 was holding true to form. No rain in sight, and still sticky-hot. I was grateful for air conditioning as I packed a garment bag. My sister, Frankie, had invited me to accompany her to Charlottesville, then on to Williamsburg to visit her children. Jessica was a University of Virginia freshman, Charlottesville, and Spencer, a third-year Southwest Virginia Community College transfer student at the college of William and Mary, Williamsburg.

I felt excited, the way I did in my younger days when Frankie and I planned trips. We always had fun, giggling about nothing in particular.

Frankie and I left at 3:30 p.m. Not a cloud in the sky — a perfectly beautiful day. We were in high spirits, telling each other, "It's just nice to get away." We inserted a '60s Motown CD, and cruised down the highway.

As we reminisced, the hours flew by. It suddenly dawned on me to ask Frankie if she'd had her car serviced. This was law for my husband and me, never travel long distances unless our vehicle was given the green light.

Frankie frowned, "What do you mean, serviced?"

"I mean, did you take your car to a reputable service center and have the oil, tires, and windshield wipers checked? In fact, have the attendant check for all things you hope won't go wrong with a car while you're driving."

Frankie's frown deepened as she snapped, "Haze, you worry too much!"

"Better safe than sorry. A stitch in time . . ."

I was cut off in mid-sentence as Frankie yelled, "Shut up! And let me drive. Change that CD! I'm tired of Marvin Gaye."

"Jones' *He Stopped Loving Her Today* was kicking into high gear when the first huge drops of rain hit Frankie's Grand Prix.

Lighting a cigarette, she groaned, "I'm not believing this. You bring an umbrella?"

"Not even a jacket."

Abruptly, it seemed, Frankie was having difficulty seeing the road. "I believe God opened up the heavens, but I wish He'd waited until Monday," she said.

"Well, just as long as He holds this car together," I commented. "It sure wouldn't be the ideal time for the wipers. . ."

Plop! Plop!

"What is that?" I yelled over the terrifying noise. "Did we have a tire blow?"

"No!" Frankie frantically screamed. "The wipers—they're out!"

I grabbed Frankie's cigarettes. I hadn't smoked in fifteen years, but suddenly it seemed a good idea.

Frankie slowed the car.

"Haze, roll your window down, look out and tell me where we're going."

"Are you crazy? I just had my hair done today!"

"Do it!"

I pushed the button. My window came down and my head went out—out into the wet, dark, unfamiliar territory of a super highway just outside Williamsburg, Virginia.

I tried to the best of my ability to direct Frankie to the shoulder of the road.

Once there, she pushed the emergency button on the car. We just sat there waiting for help that didn't present itself.

Then Frankie looked at me, really looked at me. She began laughing so hard tears streamed.

"Miss Priss, your hairdo is a little damp."

"Well, next time *I'll* drive, and *you* stick your head out the window!"

Growing serious, Frankie asked, "What are we going to do? Everyone is just driving by, totally ignoring us."

Choking on a newly lit cigarette, I moaned, "Sure could use a cell phone."

"Well, we don't have one, so think of something else."

"I'm thinking! I'm thinking!"

"Let's pull off the main drag, and try to make it to the exit. We may have to stay the night because this rain is not letting up."

Again, I leaned out the window and directed Frankie to the exit. We crept off the exit ramp and parked. Cold and shivering, I wondered if my hair would ever be the same.

To pass the time Frankie and I told stories. This kept us calm. Finally, after what seemed hours of waiting, a woman pulled beside us and asked if she could help. I wanted to hug her. We explained our situation, and she promised to call the police.

Fifteen minutes later, a canine cop wagon stopped, and a young trooper approached our car. He talked with us for a while, assessing our situation. He then walked to his vehicle, and returning, handed me a squeegee. He instructed me to lean out as far as possible in order to keep the windshield clear.

I just looked at him, and in a firm voice said, "No way am I going to Williamsburg hanging out a car window with a squeegee in my hand cleaning a windshield. I may look like a sister to The Three Stooges, but I'll be darned if I act like one!"

Trying not to laugh, the trooper warned, "Ma'am, that's the only alternative. I'll drive slowly and, with you clearing the windshield, you should be all right."

Frankie tried to reassure me, "Haze, lean out as far as you can. I promise I'll just creep along."

Gripping my squeegee, and wanting to beat Frankie over the head for not having the sense to have her car serviced, I warned her, "I don't trust you. You'd better not make any unexpected moves."

During that nightmarish three-mile-drive into Williamsburg, Frankie kept saying things like, "Lean over a little further. Better use the squeegee on your glasses. How's the weather out there? It's nice in here. Love that hairstyle, but where's the bounce?"

I'd like to bounce her, I thought. Like all the Hales, she could carry on a conversation without needing another person.

All the while I was working to keep the windshield cleared; I guess Frankie was wise cracking just to keep our minds off the situation. I don't know how she drove, or for that matter, how I hung out that window without killing myself.

Up front, the trooper was doing as he promised. Driving slowly. But those darn dogs were having one heck of a time. The van was rocking. Must be fighting, I thought.

When I saw the lights of our motel, my tears mingled with rain. My joy turned to dismay, however, as I noticed several people standing in front of the office. Spencer included. I raised my chin and pretended indifference, acted as if I did this every day. I even waved my squeegee.

The dogs had gotten louder, the rain heavier. The trooper helped Frankie and me from the car. We introduced him to Spencer, who, while extending his hand, asked, "What have they done now?" I wanted to choke him.

The trooper explained our plight, and insisted on seeing us to our room. At the door, Frankie and I thanked him. "Before you go," I queried, "I want to ask you one more thing. What is wrong with those dogs? I've never heard dogs fight like that."

Shaking his head, the young man replied, "There's only one dog in that wagon, ma'am."

Spencer chuckled as he looked at us, "Is his name Hale? One Hale can make as much to-do as the whole family gathered!"

The Case of the Missing Cat

The trouble began years ago, when like their mother and aunt before them, my niece, Jessica, and her brother, Spencer, adopted stray animals. I can never remember them without a pet. Dogs and a slew of hamsters, turtles and rabbits came and went, but cats were the constant.

Their first was a Siamese cat. Yes, an adopted Siamese named Dixie. Dixie's favorite perch was the top of the refrigerator. She pounced, to Jessica and Spencer's delight, on unsuspecting visitors, including yours truly.

Their love for cats continued into their adult years. During 1998 while Spencer lived in Norfolk, Virginia earning his Master's Degree in Art Therapy from Eastern Medical School, he adopted a black and white kitten from a local animal shelter. He and Lily the cat shared an apartment with another student, Curt. Curt had never owned a pet or had much experience with animals. Although he liked Lily, he was always kind of uneasy around her.

Once, when Spencer was away, Lily, shall we say, developed an urge to roam. Curt became really worried as Lily's behavior grew more and more erratic.

So upset was he that he dialed a veterinarian, whose number he located in the yellow pages of the telephone directory. While thumbing through the pages, running down the veterinarians, Lily wailed and rubbed against his leg.

Locating a number, Curt urgently explained Lily's behavior, even bringing her to the phone in order for the veterinarian to hear her pitiful wailing.

Dead silence.

No comment from the veterinarian. "Sir," Curt finally gasped, "what is wrong with Lily?"

"Son," came the amused reply, "sounds to me as if your cat's in heat, but I'm only guessing. You need to contact your veterinarian. You've reached the *Veterans* Administration Building!"

Spencer howled louder than Lily as Curt related this to him. The next day Spencer promptly made an appointment with a veterinarian and had Lily "fixed."

Spencer earned his Master's degree shortly after this and accepted employment as an Art Therapist at John Randolph Center in Hopewell, Virginia. He moved to Chester, about twenty minutes from Jessica, now a first-year-student at the Medical College of Virginia.

Poor Lily was almost "fixed" again. Spencer was scheduled to attend an Art Therapy conference in Orlando, Florida. Always before, when traveling, he could depend on Curt to cat-sit Lily. However, after graduation, Curt had gotten employment in another state so he wasn't available.

Saturday afternoon Spencer telephoned Jessica. Uneasy that her cat, Sunday, and her roommate's dog, Peanut, wouldn't welcome Lily, Jessica hesitated.

"She'll be fine," Spencer assured her. "I trust you completely."

"But Spence," a worried Jessica continued, "Lily hasn't been with animals. There's just been you."

Spencer chuckled, "Say no more!"

"Joke if you will, but I'm worried."

"I can't put her in a shelter. She was so pitiful when I adopted her. Besides, I wouldn't leave her with you if I felt there would be a problem. She knows you, Jess. She likes you."

"Oh, all right! Bring her on over, and you'd better bring food and litter!"

Monday night, Spencer and Lily arrived at Jessica's door. Chaos erupted. Sunday hissed and ran in circles while Peanut barked loud enough to wake the dead. Lily dived underneath a chair, thinking the shelter hadn't been such a bad place after all. Spencer deposited food and litter on a nearby sofa and quickly exited.

As Jessica left for class Tuesday morning, her roommate assured her that everything would be fine. True, it had taken half the night, but the three animals seemed to be communicating, if you called hissing and spitting communicating.

Seven hours later, Jessica returned. She'd been weary when she left for the day, and was now ready to flop in the nearest chair. Sunday and Peanut met her, bright eyed and unusually happy. Discarding her coat, Jessica called Lily. Probably hiding, Jessica surmised as she headed toward the kitchen hoping to find a prepared meal.

Instead she found her roommate pacing the floor. Between groans, Jessica learned that Lily had escaped through the back door that afternoon and hadn't returned. Jessica's heart went into overdrive as she said over and over, "Spence will kill me. He loves that cat. Spence will kill me. This is Tuesday—he'll be back Sunday."

Jessica had joined her roommate and the two of them paced side by side. Jessica suddenly stopped and warned Rachael, "Don't answer any calls from Florida! I'll call Mom and Aunt Hazel. Maybe they'll know what to do."

I told her to grab ol' Sunday, spray paint her black and white, stuff her into Lily's carrier and pray.

Frankie told her to look on the bright side. "Just think," she said, "when Spencer marries and he and his wife have children, you'll *never* be asked to baby-sit."

Jessica had one hundred fliers printed. She walked the streets shaking a bag of Meow Mix, calling Lily while curious neighbors looked on. And she did pray. A lot.

By Thursday night, there was still no sign of Lily. Armed with more fliers, Jessica stepped out the back door. There sat Lily perched on the porch banisters.

Jessica cautiously approached Lily and speaking softly, asked, "Lily, where in the world have you been?"

Lily daintily washed her white paws and answered, "Meow!"

Jessica later told us it looked as if Lily was bathed in light. "I truly believe," she stated, "God answered my prayers and guided her to safety. How else could a cat have found her way through Richmond's busy streets?"

Jessica never said a word to Spencer. She just lined Lily's carrier with the fliers!

Frankie and me with pets — 1958

Spencer and Jess with pets—1982

Veiled Memories

"Come in! Where have you been so long?"

Ninety-four-year-old Stella Stiltner lay in a hospital bed. She was supported by two large pillows which had been placed behind her back. I pulled a chair close to the bed, and before sitting, offered my assistance. She was struggling with a cup filled with hot coffee. Frightened that her trembling hands could not hold the cup, I reached to support her. She immediately pulled away and told me, "No thanks. I'm just fine."

I smiled as I eased into the old latter-back cane-bottom chair, the same chair my childish body had folded into when I came with my mother to visit. Now several years and several pounds later, caution was the rule of the day.

She's still the feisty old thing I remember, I thought.

"So, how's everything?" I asked.

"Well, how do you reckon they are?" she threw at me. "Trussed up like a hog, wearing all these tubes—one in my nose—another at the other end. I'm wore out, Hazel."

I'd been told Stella's mind was failing her, so I said a silent prayer of thanks that the reports were wrong. I carefully maneuvered the old chair closer to the bed. While Shelby, her live-in help removed the lunch tray, I looked around Stella's bedroom. Everything was the same, almost. She'd never gotten around to having a closet door installed. Instead, curtains hung on a rope stretched across the opening. Her bedroom furniture was bought in 1922 when she and her late husband, Arlie married. I glanced at the floor and was shocked to see the same faded cracked lino-leum on which I'd played almost 45 years ago.

Her walls, however, were no longer bare. There were several beautifully framed photographs of Arlie and her invalid son, Lacy. Jesus Christ looked at me from every angle: framed pictures of Him as a child, the Lamb crucified and finally as the risen Savior.

I observed too, that scattered among various sized medicine bottles angels kept a silent vigil; some kneeling and some standing with wide spread wings.

I'd known Stella my whole life, had grown up living next door to her, and during her lingering illness I'd visited several times. Why, then, was I seeing all this as if for the first time?

Shelby, after cleaning the lunch tray, motioned me outside the room. Once outside Stella's astonishingly clear hearing range, she again cautioned me, "Since your last visit, Stella's mind ain't quite right, so don't pay any attention to her." I assured her that Stella and I would be just fine, and stepped inside Stella's room only to find her snoozing. Once again, I eased into the creaky old chair.

She opened her eyes wide and looked at me. "Been across the road to your Dad's old place?"

"No, what do you think of it, Stella?"

"Oh, honey, I think it's beautiful. Don't you?"

"It looks fine. I'll bet Dad's turned several times in his grave, though, especially if he got a good look at that big Sears fence stretched all around the place. He always said he'd never put up a fence to keep himself in and his neighbors out."

"What do you think about all of Jo Ann's flowers? Don't it remind you of them pretty flowers your Granny Combs kept planted in buckets around the porch?"

"Jo Ann has the same knack with flowers, but I'm guessing she won't paint all her containers a wild and crazy pink the way Granny did. Remember?"

Stella began laughing so hard Shelby came running and sternly warned me not to upset her.

Stella just as forcefully told Shelby to mind her own business, and while she was at it, to find her dark glasses.

I giggled when she slipped on those dark glasses and threw her long braided silver-white hair across her right shoulder.

"It's good to hear you laugh," she began. "When your mother, then your dad died, I worried about you more than the other two sisters. I know they were just as hurt, but they didn't live as close as you. You never missed a day comin' back up on this old hill. It broke your heart the place was sold, didn't it?"

I started to answer, but her head dropped on the pillow and she again drifted off. As before, she awoke with a start and picked up on our unfinished conversation.

"What you need is to have a good talk with your mother."

Oh, brother, here it comes. Her mind is doing crazy things. Why hadn't I left as she slept? I decided rather than upset her to play along.

"Have you talked with *your* mother, Stella?"

"Oh, honey, lots of times. She was mad at me though, and didn't come around until I promised her me and Lacy would be buried beside her and not up on the mountain with Arlie. The first time she visited she was wearing her grave clothes: a purple dress, but the oddest thing, she was wearing a wide-brim picture hat. She'd made herself a veil out of the same material her dress was, you know, that gauzy stuff. She came walking back of the house one Sunday June morning. I was standing at the sink washing quart jars when I saw her. I dropped the jar I was holding and it broke into a million pieces. I leaned out the window, and I don't know why, but I wasn't afraid anymore."

"Mother, what are you doing wearing that veil?"

"It's Sunday, and I'm going to church. Stella, I raised you to not work on Sunday and here you are, washing jars. You stop that right now!"

"Mother, don't fuss at me. You know I can't leave Lacy. I've got cucumber pickles ready to can, and had to get these jars ready."

"Well, it ain't right. The good Lord ain't pleased and I'm not either."

"Mother, before you leave, promise me you will uncover your face. You must show that pretty skin and let people see you."

I hurriedly asked, "How many times has she visited since?"

"Honey, she came to me this morning. She told me she'd talked to your mother yesterday. Said Effie told her you'd be coming by. I wasn't a bit surprised to see you."

"Did she say how Mom was doing?"

"Oh, bustlin' about, tellin' everybody what to do. She said Effie liked her veil so much, she asked her to make one for her. She did too, except Effie's was pink to match her grave clothes."

"So, your mother didn't listen to you about lifting her veil?"

"Why no, she just sewed another one, only fuller this time. She told me she already had one made for me, wanted to know what color my grave clothes would be. I told her pink, like Effie's."

Hidden as she was behind dark glasses, I felt, rather than saw Stella's piercing gaze as she asked me, "Do you want one?"

"No, I'll make do with what I have, Stella. I never did like veils, didn't even wear one on my wedding day."

She reached out for me, and I took her small, cold, feeble hands. I felt incredible sadness as I looked at this shadow of a once vital woman. I leaned over, kissed her and assured her I'd be back in a few days.

I'd almost reached the door when she said in a loud, clear voice. "When you talk to your mother, tell her I'll soon be with her, and, Hazel, see to it my grave clothes are pink. Mother has my veil ready."

I blew a kiss and through tears, promised her I'd honor her wishes.

As I drove down the hill, I kept thinking about Stella. She was already wearing that invisible veil; at least it partially covered her face. One side of her brain, the uncovered side, saw clearly into this world, while the veiled side lived in twilight, already in the other world.

It was the twilight side I found fascinating. Some day I pray I'll see Mom again, and I'll not be surprised to see her wearing a wide-brim picture hat wrapped in gauze with a veil attached.

Stella at home — 1980s

151

Cabin Fever Conversations

January 30, 1998, the third day of uncertainty. Tuesday evening, January 27, 7:00 p.m., the power shut down. A massive snow storm dumped over two feet of wet snow throughout the mountains of Southwest Virginia, and three days later it was still snowing.

Fortunately, we had an alternative heat source. Several years earlier son Greg had gas logs installed as a Christmas gift. Without the blower in use, very little heat was distributed, but it was better than nothing. Candles burned, gas logs glowed and created a cozy romantic environment. But who wanted to become romantic with a bearded, disgruntled man wrapped in layers of clothing? I'm sure this disgruntled man felt the same about his stringy-haired, oily-faced wife clad in a terry cloth bathrobe. After John shaved and I used dry shampoo, our attitudes changed, but Island Creek telephoned. Inclement weather created unpredictable work schedules.

After John left for work, I worried as I watched red taillights fade in the distance. An hour later he telephoned that he'd made the trip across the treacherous mountain highway to Island Creek Coal Company's No. 3 mine located in neighboring Buchanan County.

I telephoned friends and family. First, my sister Frankie. I was surprised when she cheerfully answered and informed me that her electricity and television cable service weren't disturbed! Only twenty miles separated us, but that day she may as well have lived in another country. During our conversation, Frankie informed me that she had the best recipe for snow cream. Not in the mood for her gloating, I answered, "Well, mix up a batch for yourself!" I hung up to the sound of her chuckling.

I 'phoned my sister Nadine, who along with thousands of others throughout Southwest Virginia was "roughing" it. She told me that one of her husband's large barns had collapsed and killed six cows. I sympathized, and we talked a while.

Afterwards, I talked with a dear elderly friend, Vivian. She told me, "Hazel, it isn't hard for me. During the 1930s, this was commonplace. Of course, after getting used to the luxury of evenly distributed heat, it's different. Remember though, I kept my old wood-burning stove, and my son brought a load of wood, so Daffy and I are warm and have plenty to eat. Don't worry about us." I heard Daffy meowing in the background as if to confirm that all was well.

A knock on the door interrupted our conversation. It was a neighbor with news he'd received that telephone use was prohibited except for emergencies.

After he left, I made a list of everything I needed to do, and then threw it away. What I really needed was people. I dreaded removing my warm robe, but I found John's fleece-lined long handle underwear, and wore them under sweats.

John had shoveled a path to our car, and I had no trouble making my way to it. I used a broom to sweep the top before sliding behind the wheel. The underwear sure felt good as I sat inside a cold car and waited for the heater to do its job. I kept thinking I wished my husband had some place other than our garage to keep his prized 1990 Lincoln Continental Mark VII Special Edition. Then again, if I'd used an ounce of common sense, I would have started the engine minutes ago and gone back inside the house to stay warm. Instead, I sat there shivering and shaking. I credited John's underwear for saving my life!

Hoping that Little General Grocery and Deli wasn't closed, I cautiously backed out of our driveway and maneuvered the slippery highway.

I found the locals seated in the deli section around tables decorated with candles propped in upside down paper cups. A hole had been cut in the bottom of each and a candle inserted. Bradley Strouth, never without comment, yelled as I came through the door. "Haze, I'd be ashamed sending old John out to work on a day like today."

I countered with one of my more believable lies because everyone knew how frugal my daddy had been. "Bradley, my daddy left me enough money until we'll never need to work another day. John works because he wants to."

Bradley dropped like one of the paper cup candles.

Jack Ray asked, "Bradley, you'll get smart with her again, won't you?

Butch Honaker interrupted, "Grab a chair and sit a while!"

I grew up with these people, and it felt good to get out of the house and gab.

The store's generator was up and running, so I ordered a bowl of homemade vegetable soup. I ate the soup slowly, savoring it as the good-natured bantering continued.

Dennis Whited grinned his shy smile. "You know, I hear the governor might declare all of Southwest Virginia a disaster area. Hell, it's been a disaster area for forty years. They're just now gettin' around to tellin' everybody."

Conversation flowed with everyone adding memories of how things used to be during frigid mountain winters: cold linoleum-covered floors, grate fires, wood-burning stoves, snow blowing through single-paned windows, and seeing our breath freeze.

We all agreed that we had become like the soft and spoiled younger generation—a generation, for the most part, of whiners who just could not cope without electronic gadgets, television, computers, microwave ovens, and a car by the time they turned sixteen.

I nodded when Butch remarked, "If it wasn't such a burden on the elderly and sick, I'd like to see this continue for a couple of months. It would be a lesson in survival, and teach us to get back to the basics."

Subconsciously though, I remembered my frustration over having to sit in a cold automobile. I recalled as a child how I walked and waded snow up to my waist because my daddy never owned a vehicle. I'm no better than the younger generation I labeled "whiners," I thought as I wrapped my hands around a still-warm coffee cup.

We talked a bit longer, then I said my goodbyes and paid for my rations — two Mars bars, two Reese's peanut butter cups, and two soft drinks.

"Loadin' up on that comfort food, ain't you, sis?" store manager Paul Hughes kidded as I paid at the counter.

As I left the store, feeling much better than when I arrived, I threw over my shoulder, "Bradley, I won't spend *all* my inheritance in one place!"

Remembering Hearth & Home

Frank Hale's Grocery and Delivery Service

My paternal grandparents, Robert Franklin and Ida Belle Breedlove Hale, were well-known Russell County residents. Granny Hale was a church-going, hardworking woman who bore my grandfather ten children. Grandpa Hale struggled to provide for his large family by farming a section of inherited land in the Gardner section of the county.

He wanted to better provide for the family, so he took the plunge, invested his hard earned savings, and became partners with Granny Hale's cousin, Perry Herndon. The two purchased a small building in the old section of Swords Creek across from the train depot and established a grocery business. At this time, mid 1920s, Swords Creek was a busy place with passenger and freight trains arriving and leaving daily.

The grocery business flourished.

In 1939, Mr. Herndon sold his interest to Grandpa. Within a few months, Grandpa relocated to a recently vacated two-story building located just above the spot where the Swords Creek Elementary School now stands.

This large space afforded Grandpa a chance to expand. Shelves lined both sides of the room, with counter space running alongside these shelves. One counter top was used primarily for stocking dry goods, such as rolls of material and cooking utensils. The other counter top held the cash register and provided

Grandpa a place to order supplies from traveling salesmen and do what he most enjoyed, chat with his customers.

One staple for each counter was a glass container filled with candy. Grandpa saw that these were never empty. Every child who ventured inside his store received free candy.

Brown sugar was stored in wooden barrels, and a metal bread rack occupied a spot between the counters. A potbellied coal and wood-fed stove stood at the back of the store.

Hazel Dye Miller, who as a young girl was employed at the store, related to me that this was a favorite spot for Granny Hale. Granny sat in a large rocking chair and during winter months tended the fire. While seated in that old rocker, she read her Bible and delighted in sharing God's word with customers. Then at day's end, Grandpa and his friends claimed this favorite spot and played checkers until way into the night.

When enough people complained they had no way of getting to the store, my grandfather purchased a truck, installed gas tanks, and established the first grocery delivery service in the area.

1939 was an unforgettable year for the people living in and around Swords Creek. Frank Hale's Grocery Service now read Frank Hale's Grocery and Delivery Service.

Youngest daughter, Opal, helped keep store accounts, and her husband, Jim Honaker, assisted with delivery. Grandpa Hale traveled rough back roads all up and down the hills and hollows each Tuesday taking orders. He and Jim delivered these orders the following Saturday morning. Thelma Johnson Barrett told me "Mr. Hale always put a little poke of free candy in with mother's groceries for us children."

I never knew my grandfather. A sudden and unexpected heart attack took him from this earth in 1944. But through the stories told to me by those who did know him, I feel honored to be his granddaughter. He never refused credit to anyone in need. He tipped his hat to ladies, always. He was resourceful and enterprising. He knew how to have fun. He loved children.

My paternal grandparents, Robert Franklin and Ida Belle (Breedlove) Hale
Swords Creek, early 1940s

Cable Connection

as told to me by cousin Harry Moore

Folks living along the Clinch River in the Gardner Section of Russell County, Virginia during the summer of 1923 were talking nonstop about Frazier Hale's invention.

And it was keeping his 14-year-old nephew Beach awake at night.

Frazier's farm bordered that of Beach's parents, Frank and Belle Hale. Frank was proprietor of two thriving grocery stores in the Swords Creek area, leaving Beach and his younger brother, Slemp, to operate his small farm. The boys were good workers, and once work on their farm was completed, their uncle Frazier sometimes hired them to help with inevitable problems occurring on his larger working farm. A wagon wheel would break spokes or an axel, a mowing machine would run over a rock and break a blade, a horse would lose his metal shoe and need to be shod, a cow got sick, and on and on.

Beach had a natural talent to deal with these problems. He saw possibilities and solutions, too, just like his uncle Frazier. He felt Frazier's invention was *the* supreme challenge.

Part of Frazier's farm stretched up a mountain and the land was level, so Frazier raised crops up there. But he had a problem getting his crops down the mountain.

His solution was to stretch a metal cable from the barn on top of the mountain to his barn near the home place. He attached a pulley on to the cable allowing the crops to be pulled down to the barn below.

Along with hard work and curiosity, Beach had an adventurous air that was sparked with courage and spunk. He began bragging that he would ride the cable off the mountain. His brothers, sisters and numerous cousins immediately challenged him to make true his brags.

Even though he didn't have a clue how to do it, he couldn't refuse a challenge. So he lay awake at night figuring out how to do it.

After a restless night, Beach approached his uncle Frazier. He straightened his slim shoulders, stood straight, and removed his battered cap from his thick hair before stating, "Uncle Frazier, I'm gonna ride that cable off the mountain!"

Frazier had been bent over hoeing corn. He rose slowly, reached into a back pocket of his denim overalls, removed a large handkerchief and wiped perspiration from his face. He replaced his handkerchief, laid aside the hoe, and slowly sprinkled Prince Albert tobacco from a drawstring pouch on to thin white paper. He carefully rolled a cigarette, wet the paper, twisted the ends, and struck a match.

Beach fidgeted, thinking he could make the ride from the mountaintop in less time than it took his uncle to roll a cigarette.

Frazier took a draw or two before commenting, "Why, Beach, you'll get killed on that thing!"

"But Uncle Frazier, I've thought about this a whole lot. I'm gonna make a large leather seat that will be plenty strong to hold me. Besides that, I'm going to use one of them two stacks of hay you got close to the barn down here. See, when I come down the mountain and the cable dips toward the Clinch, then starts up the hill toward the barn, it will slow up enough to let me slip out of my leather seat. I'll plunge into the haystack. My forward motion will be slowed enough to stop me."

164

Beach, in his excitement, was walking all over Frazier's just-hoed corn stalks.

Frazier reached out and grabbed his nephew. "Slow down, son! If you don't stop prancin' all over my corn, you're going to need a leather seat, but not for riding! Besides, what's Frank and Belle gonna say about this?"

Beach stopped and mumbled an apology. Frazier picked up his hoe, and was ready to resume work, but Beach kept on talking. "Uncle Frazier, hear me out! I'm not finished."

Frazier pulled his sweat stained old straw hat lower, and leaned on the hoe handle. "Son, I believe you'd worry fleas off a dog. Now, I ain't got all day."

Beach, talking fast, continued, "I'm gonna stuff my trousers and shirt sleeves with a lot of dried clover hay to help soften the landing. And I'm wearing airplane goggles and a helmet, and a pair of long leather boots. I can get these things from Daddy's stores."

Frazier, not even attempting to hide a grin, commented, "Well, Beach, I believe you got it pretty well figured. Go Ahead! *If* Frank and Belle says it's okay."

Frank Hale was amused at the whole idea. He agreed Beach would be safe while providing much needed entertainment for the communities of Gardner, Swords Creek, and Honaker. He placed announcements of the event in both his stores.

Belle Hale, a devout Christian, worried herself sick, and asked her church members to pray for her son.

The big day arrived, and Frazier Hale's property was crowded with folks attending from all over. Frazier's daughters sold coffee and fried pies, and people commented that this was more fun than a church social. However, some privately wondered what tragedy might befall Beach.

Meanwhile, Beach prepared himself. He asked his mother to say a word of prayer as he stuffed his sleeves and trousers. He tried to conceal his shaking hands as he pulled on a pair of old leather work gloves.

Slemp rode with him on one of their father's saddle horses to the top of the mountain.

The stage was set!

Slemp had a rough time squeezing Beach into the leather seat because he was so bulky from all the clothes and stuffing.

Beach was so keyed up he almost forgot his helmet and goggles he'd placed in the saddlebags, but Slemp reminded him.

Beach's heart was throbbing like a trip-hammer, but in a practiced, calm voice he said to Slemp, "Push me off!"

"God be with you, Beach!" yelled Slemp as he gave him a mighty shove.

Beach needed that blessing, and his almost-forgotten goggles.

He rapidly gained speed, and had he not had those goggles, he couldn't have seen a thing. He was drawing too near the cliffs that jutted from the mountain, but because his eyes were covered and protected, he was able to judge how close he was coming to hitting them. He quickly raised his legs as high as possible, barely missing the ragged sharp cliff edge.

He sped on.

The cable dipped toward the river, then started to rise toward the barn. Beach's momentum slowed enough for him to release himself. He plunged into the haystack, and his forward motion was slowed greatly just as he'd planned. But not quite enough to prevent him from plunging straight through that hay stack into a huge mud puddle under it.

Sopping wet, muddy, and extremely happy, Beach strutted through the crowd. He hugged Slemp, and told him, "We did it, little brother!"

Belle was so happy, she shouted her praise to the Lord. Frank kept saying, "He's a Hale, all right!"

Friends and relatives clapped each other on the back. "I knew he could do it," his cousin Blanche said to her sister Dorothy.

Dorothy grinned before commenting, "Then how come I heard you bet against him? You bet Daisy a quarter her brother wouldn't get half-way down the mountain."

"Did not!"

"Did so!"

The girls stopped arguing as a now clean Beach swaggered toward them. "We're going to Daddy's store out near the train depot. Ya'll comin'?"

Everyone spent the remainder of the day at Frank's store. The large store porch was a perfect place for friends to greet friends. Both the visitors and storeowner profited greatly. Hard working people forgot their troubles and enjoyed the day.

And as his cash register jingled, Frank said to Frazier, "Brother, I like to see people come together the way they have today."

Frazier pulled down two Prince Albert tins from a shelf before answering, "Yeah, Frank, it's been a wonderful day all around. There are people here I ain't seen in years, and I'm not just talking about folks who live around here. People from different counties!"

Frank dipped into a cooler filled with ice water for his favorite peach soda. He smiled at Frazier. "Guess I'd call it a *cable* connection, wouldn't you, Fraz'?"

Dad at home in Gardner, VA — 1926

Dad's sisters and nieces all dressed up for the celebration. From left: sisters Opal and Belle, and nieces Juanita and Clara

About the Author

Hazel Hale-Bostic
NOW . . .

Hazel Hale-Bostic graduated Honaker High School, class of 1964, and stayed home because that is where she wanted to be. She quotes her Dad as he sat on his Swords Creek front porch and appreciated the mountain view all around him: "Why in the world do folks want to run all over creation and back when we have everything we need right here?"

She is proud of her heritage; and began writing in order to keep it alive. True Appalachians are steeped in family values, individual pride, and what she feels is the most valuable of values — identity. "May we never lose our identity."

She comes from a long line of both storytellers and readers. As a child she couldn't wait for the annual Hale Family Reunion held at the Frazier Hale home place in the Gardner section of Russell County. The only things better than tables filled with delicious food were the stories told and re-told. Her Dad was one of the top-dog storytellers. Her mother, an avid reader, exchanged books the way her Hale in-laws swapped yarns.

Hazel writes fiction and nonfiction, and sprinkles humor into both. She has won several awards for excellence in writing, usually in the nonfiction category. Perhaps it's because readers can often hardly believe the bigger-than-life characters and the situations they are in are NOT fiction.

She has spent her entire life in these up-close-and-personal mountains. She didn't follow the great exodus from the hills of home. In her own words, "I loved home then. I love home now."

Home is where you feel like somebody.
Lee Smith

. . . and THEN

CREDITS

The Bluestone Review

1. "An Uncommon Woman"—published 2001
2. "Warm Morning Memories"—published 2002
3. "Veiled Memories"—published 2008
4. "Transition"—published 2010
5. "The Poorhouse"—published 2010
6. "All Hail the Power"—published 2010
7. "A Daffodil Day"—published 2011

The Storyteller Magazine

1. "One Wild Ride"—published Oct/Nov/Dec 2002 Vol.7, Issue 4
2. "Veiled Memories"—published Jan/Feb/Mar 2003 Vol. 8, Issue 1
3. "Oh! The Shame of It"—published April/May/June 2003 Vol. 8, Issue 2
4. "Monkey Shines"—published July/Aug/Sept 2003 Vol. 8, Issue 3
5. "Estate of Confusion"—published Oct/Nov/Dec 2003 Vol. 8, Issue 4
6. "Colorful Aunt Sally"—published April/May/June 2004 Vol. 9, Issue 2
7. "Pay As You Go"—published Jan/Feb/March 2004 Vol. 9, Issue 1
8. "Wheelchair Angel"—published July, August, Sept 2004 Vol. 9, Issue 3
9. "R-E-S-P-E-C-T"—published Oct/Nov/Dec 2004 Vol. 9, Issue 4
10. "Stress Without Distress" published April/May/June 2005 Vol. 10, Issue 2
    *Received 2nd place People's Choice Award—Essay
11. "An Uncommon Woman"—July/Aug/Sept 2005 Vol. 10/Issue 3
    *Received 2nd place People's Choice Award—Nonfiction
12. "Remembering Wayne"—published Oct/Nov/Dec 2005 Vol. 10, Issue 4
    *Received 1st place People's Choice Award—Nonfiction
13. "It's Party Time"—published Jan/Feb/March 2006 Vol. 11, Issue 1
14. "The Last Chase"—published July/August/Sept 2006 Vol. 11, Issue 3
15. "Transition"—published Oct/Nov/Dec 2006 Vol. 11, Issue 4
16. "Harvesting Memories"—published July/August/Sept 2007 Vol. 12, Issue 3
17. "The Family Tree Fell on Me"—published July/August/Sept 2008 Vol. 13
    *Received 1st place People's Choice Award—Nonfiction
18. "A Few Kind Words"—published Oct/Nov/Dec 2010 Vol. 15, Issue 3
19. "Aftermath"—published Oct/Nov/Dec 2010 Vol. 15, Issue 3
    *Received 2nd place People's Choice Award—Nonfiction
20. "Saddle Oxfords and Grapevine Swings"—published Oct/Nov/Dec 2010 Vol. 15, Issue 4

Modern Mountain Magazine (M Magazine)

1. "Fox Hunting—A Family Tradition"—published Summer 1998 Vol. 3, No. 2
2. "Corncob Dynamite"—published Summer 2000 Vol. 5, No. 11
3. "Warm Morning Memories"—published Spring 2001 Vol. 6, No. 1
4. "Caught in the Middle"—published Fall 2001 Vol. 6, No III
5. "The Smokin' Frog"—published Summer 2002 Vol. 7, No II
6. "One Wild Ride"—published Summer 2003
7. "Estate of Confusion"—published Fall 2004 Vol. 9, No III
8. "Stress Without Distress"—published Winter 2005 Vol. 10, No IV
9. "Transition"—published Fall 2006 Vol. 11, No. IV
10. "The Poorhouse"—published Spring 2007 Vol. 12, No 1
11. "Wheelchair Angel"—published Summer 2009 Vol. 13, No. III
12. "All Hail the Power"—published Summer 2009 Vol. 14, No III
13. "Harvesting Memories"—published Fall 2010 Vol. 15, No IV
14. "Déjà vu"—published Summer 2011 Vol. 16, No III

The Clinch Mountain Review

1. "Cable Connection"—published 2005
2. "Frank Hale's Grocery and Delivery Service"—published 2008

Blue Ridge Traditions

1. "Letter to the Editor"—published June 2002 Vol. 9, No. 3
2. "The Smokin' Frog"—published April 2002 Vol. 9, No 1
3. "Photo Finish"—published November 2001 Vol. 8, No 10

Now & Then

1. "Colorful Aunt Sally"—published spring 1997 Vol. 14, No. 1

Reminisce Extra

1. "Cowgirls in Hog Heaven"—August, 1997 Vol. 5, No. 4
2. "Granny Combs"—published October 1998 Vol. 6, No 5
3. "Uncle Arthur's Toothache"—published April, 2000 Vol. 8, No. 2

Northern Stars

1. "Lost in Cyberspace"—published May/June 2001
2. "The 'Ruptured' Bear Chase"—published July/August 2001
3. "The Smokin' Frog"—published Nov/Dec 2001
4. "Caught in the Middle"—published May/June 2002
   *First place winner—NS quarterly Fiction Contest

5. "Estate of Confusion"—published May/June 2003
   * First place winner—*NS* quarterly Fiction Contest
6. "Wheelchair Angel"—published May/June 2004
7. "R-E-S-P-E-C-T"—published Nov/Dec 2004
8. "Transition"—published Nov/Dec 2005
9. "All Hail the Power"—published Jan/Feb 2006
   *Honorable Mention—*NS* quarterly Poetry Contest
10. "Old Rose and Me"—published May/June 2006
11. "Haiku poetry—published Nov/Dec 2006
12. "Ralphster and the Rosebush"—published Nov/Dec '07
13. "Lester's Peacock"—published May/June 2007
14. "Righteousness on Parade"—published July/August 2007
15. "Uncle Arthur's Toothache"—published Jan/Feb/March 2008
16. "The Freelanders"—published Nov/Dec 2009
17. "Déjà vu"—published Jan/Feb 2011

Sharing and Caring

1. "Corncob Dynamite"—published Vol. 6, No. 24
2. "Opening the Storehouse of Granny Memories"—published Vol. 7, No. 25
3. "Photo Finish"—published Vol. 7, No 26
4. "An Uncommon Woman"—published Vol 7. No 27
   *First Place—Best of Prose (Editors choice)
5. "People Are Indeed Funny"—published Vol. 7, No. 28
6. "Fox Hunting—A Family Tradition"—published Vol. 8, No 20
7. "Veiled Memories"—published Vol. 8, No. 30
8. "Monkey Shines"—published Vol. 9, No. 35
9. "Life Lessons Seen Through a Windshield"—published Vol. 8, No. 32
10. "So Who's Little Jimmy"—published December 2001
11. "R-E-S-P-E-C-T"—published December 2001
    *First Place—Editors Choice Award—Fiction
12. "Writing With Feeling"—published Vol. 1, Issue 2
13. "Ma Tackett's Welcome"—published Vol. 1, Issue 2

AppalTalk

1. "Remembering Granny Combs"—published Vol. 1, No. 3 Fall 1999
2. "An Uncommon Woman"—published Vol. 2, No. 2 Summer 2000
3. "Scared the Coal Dust Off"—published Vol. 2, No. 4 Winter 2001
4. "Life Lessons Seen Through a Windshield"—published Vol. 2, No 3 Fall

Sunrise
1. "The Smokin' Frog"—published Vol. 1, Issue 1 Jan. 2004
2. "The Case of the Missing Cat"—published Vol. 1, Issue 2 April 2004

Simply Words
1. "Corncob Dynamite"—published Winter 1999 Vol. 8, Issue 4

Yesterday's Magazette
1. "The Family Tree Fell on Me"—published Sept/Oct 1997 Vol. 25, No. 5

The Funny Paper
1. "The Smokin' Frog"—published No. 77
   *Received Editors Choice Award—Fiction

Seasons For Writing
1. "The Family Tree Fell On Me"—published August 2003, Issue 23
   *4th Place—Best in Prose
2. "Estate of Confusion" published—October 2003

Zeniths & Zephyrs
(A collection of short stories from various authors who call the mountains home)
MtnValy Publishing
"Colorful Aunt Sally"

Crossing Troublesome
25 years of the Appalachian Writers Workshop
1. Untitled tribute to Lee Smith—published 2002

Ruth Whitt's Russell County
1. "Appalachia's Friend and Writer: (Biography)—published 2002

Women in the Arts
1. "First Cat"—published Autumn 2005
2. "Cats at the Veterans Admin"—published Autumn 2006

Cameo's Best of Winter Poetry
"Transition"—published 2005

Front Porch Monthly
1. "Veiled Memories"—Spring 2008
2. "Wheelchair Angel"—Summer 2008
3. "Cowgirls in Hog Heaven"—Autumn 2008
4. "Monkey Shines"—Winter 2008

5. "Warm Morning Memories"—Spring 2009
6. "Uncle Arthur's Toothache"—Spring 2009
7. "Frank Hale's Grocery and Delivery Service"—March 2009
8. "A Few Kind Words"—May 2009
9. "The Last Chase"—June 2009
10. "The Poorhouse"—July 2009
11. "One Wild Ride"—August 2009
12. "The Case of the Missing Cat"—September 2009
13. "Old Rose and Me"—October 2009
14. "Transition"—November 2009
15. "All Hail the Power"—March 2010
16. "Saddle Oxfords and Grapevine Swings"—May 2010
17. "An Appalachian Woman's Journey"—June 2010
18. "Remembering By Ginger"—October 2010
19. "Uptown Girl"—December 2010
20. "Hot Coffee and Warm Memories"—January 2011
21. "Ralphster and the Rosebush"—March 2011
22. "Trashed Teeth"—April 2011
23. "Bells and Barn Lofts"—May 2011
24. "Déjà vu"—June 2011
25. "Barber Shop Saturday Mornings" July 2011

Creative Writing Contest Awards

1. Third Place Adult Essay Contest—Chautauqua Creative Writing Contest (June 2004)
2. Third Place Adult Essay Contest—Chautauqua Creative Writing Contest (June 2005)
3. Third Place Adult Essay Contest—Chautauqua Creative Writing Contest (June 2007)
4. Third Place Adult Essay Contest—The 2002 Virginia Highlands Festival
5. Second Place Adult Essay Contest—The 2006 Virginia Highlands Festival
6. First Place Adult Essay Contest—The Appalachian Heritage Writers Symposium (June 2011)
7. Second Place Adult Essay Contest—Chautauqua Creative Writing Contest (June 2011)